Dedicated to William B. Tucker, Sr., my father, my friend, and my model for loving Christ.

The author wishes to express his heartfelt gratitude to all those who have taken of their valuable time to edit this material and offer suggestions to make this book better. All errors and mistakes in this book are my own. The author would be indebted to any reader who, so desiring, wishes to send corrections to him at reformedbaptistpress@gmail.com.

AGAPE: THE

ESSENCE OF SAVING

FAITH

AN EXPOSITIONAL

DEFINITION

NATHAN W. TUCKER

1689

Reformed Baptist Press

TABLE OF CONTENTS

PREFACE

What is so important about the topic of saving faith that warrants an entire book? It is because the question of what constitutes saving faith goes to the very the heart of the Gospel. It doesn't matter how theologically sound my presentation of the Gospel message is if I also cannot present a theologically sound call to repentance and faith. If, in response to the question, "What must we do to be saved?" (Acts 16:20; see also Acts 2:37)), I have no answer, I have no business holding myself out as a minister of the Gospel.

And in the America of the twenty-first century, the Gospel is under tremendous attack. Not so much in how it is presented, but in the response that it calls for in its listeners. First, it under attack by the widespread practice of easy-believism in which no actual conversion takes place. Rather, the preacher simply asks for a token response in which listeners raise their hands, or walk the aisle to the alter, or fill out a card in the pew. And if any counseling of souls takes place, it is only to have the individual recite a prayer before they are pronounced to the rest of the congregation as saved. This type of response is no where found in Scripture or the practice of the church for the first 1800 years, and it has lead to devastating results wherever it is practiced. For we have millions of professing believers in this country alone, especially in the Deep South, who believe that they are saved because of a profession of faith made once upon a time when, in fact, they remain on the road to hell. But it is nearly impossible to convince them of that, because in their dead, blind, and hardened sin nature they have persuaded themselves that they have punched their get-out-of-hell free card and can now continue to live like the devil. They think they got their vaccination, so they sin with the best of them and think they will still escape the fires of hell.

Secondly, the Gospel call is under attack by prosperity Gospel preachers who hold Christ out as nothing less than a sugar daddy. "Come to Christ," they say, "and He will give you the desires of your heart. You want health? Come to Christ! You want prosperity? Come to Christ! You want power? Come to Christ! Whatever you want, name it and claim it in Christ and He will give it to you! Come to Christ to live your best life now!" If I ever utter those words, cast me out of the church post haste as a heretic. God is not a genie in the bottle. He is not a sugar daddy. He is not Santa Clause. He no where promisees you your best life now. Rather, He promises that if you want to keep your life now you will lose it (Matt. 16:25). The prosperity Gospel is a diabolical Gospel that has no bases in Scripture whatsoever. All it produces are false converts who use God to worship the god of themselves and the desires of their own heart.

Third, the Gospel call is under attack by a milder version of the prosperity gospel which I call the Good Life Gospel.. The clearest example of this that I've been able to come up with is from the movie *Unbroken: Path to Redemption*, the sequel to *Unbroken: The Unbelievable True Story*. Both are good movies and should be watched back-to-back. However, when the movie portrays Louie Zamperini's conversion at a Billy Graham crusade, the preacher who played Billy Graham (Will Graham, the famous evangelist's grandson) kept appealing to Christ as the answer to all the brokenness in people's lives: "You have a bad marriage, come to Christ! You have problems with your kids, come to Christ! You have financial problems, come to Christ! You have an addiction, come to

Christ!" (paraphrasing). In fact, in the movie Billy Graham's character even promised his listeners that, "all your problems will be solved" by accepting Christ. Such a blasphemous message (Job; Acts 14:22; Rom. 8:17; 1 Thess. 3:3; 2 Tim. 3:12; 1 Pet. 2:20-21, 4:12) is merely the milder step-brother of the prosperity gospel, differing from it only by degree. It doesn't offer health, wealth, and power, simply a quite, peaceful life without trouble or hardship. But it is no less evil and despicable because it offers Christ as a sugar daddy who will give you a middle class lifestyle rather than the billionaire lifestyle that it's more glamorous step-brother proclaims.

For these reasons, this topic is a matter of eternal life or eternal death. Saving faith is not whether you believe the Gospel, but rather whether you love the Gospel. Saving faith is not having head knowledge about God, but rather is enjoying God. Saving faith is not coming to Christ for what He does for you, but because you find Him irresistibly beautiful. Saving faith is not coming to Christ for His toys, but because you are passionate to magnify His glory.

In this adaptation of a sermon series I gave several years ago, we will examine five reasons why love for God must be an essential component of saving faith:

1. Because the totality of Scripture defines it that way —as a coming and tasting, a receiving and loving, a seeing and treasuring, a drinking and enjoying the Person of Christ.

2. Because God exists as a Trinity, saving faith must, of necessity, partake of the overflow of joyous love that the Triune God has in and of Himself.

3. Because only faith that loves God can possibly glorify God.

4. Because godly sorrow over sin leading to genuine saving penitent faith can only be grounded in love for God.

5. Because only love-fueled faith perseveres until the end.

Nathan W. Tucker
Omaha Indian Reservation
Winter 2025

1 SAVING FAITH IS RECEIVING CHRIST AS YOUR TREASURE

*I*n this chapter we are going to focus on the Apostle John's definition of saving faith as a faith that treasures Christ supremely:

> 12 But as many *as did receive Him*, to them He gave authority to become sons of God, to those *believing in His name*: 13 who were begotten, not of bloods, nor of the will of flesh, nor of the will of man, but of God.
>
> (Jn. 1:10-13 NYLT; emphasis added)

First, however, we need to understand how we as humans are wired; what motivates us to do the things we do. None of us behave in a vacuum. We are not androids like Data on *Star Trek* consisting of artificial intelligence but no emotions. Rather, we behave out of desire for delight. We do things because we want to do them because we think they will bring us happiness. We are motivated by a domineering self-love to do things in order to maximize our pleasure. We are self-indulgent, pleasure-seeking creatures in the relentless, insatiable pursuit of joy.

So, for instance, if you have a sixteen year old son who you just caught drinking and driving with his friends on a Saturday night, how are you going to persuade him not to do it again? One approach would be to try to frighten the desire to party out of him. You could make him watch videos of car accidents and dead bodies caused by drunk drivers. You could have him go to the hospital to meet victims of drunk driving accidents. You could warn him of the dire criminal charges he risks. Or tell him of the huge financial awards a jury might order him to pay a victim in a civil lawsuit. You could warn him of the dangers of alcoholism and have him talk with drunks on the street and in shelters.

A second approach would be to convince him that his desires for partying are wrong and should be denied. Call it the Stoic approach of self-denial. Or the Vulcan approach of emotionless logic. You could try to persuade him that his desires for friends, popularity, and having a good time are wrong and that he must suppress them. You could seek to convince him that he must go through life emotionless. That if he is having a good time it is a vice. That if he is enjoying himself it is a sin. That only a self-denying, emotionless life in which you only do what you do not want to do is virtuous.

A third approach would be legalism—to fill his world with rules and regulations in hopes of suppressing his desires for friends, popularity, and a good time. You could have him attend AA meetings. You could limit his cell phone use. You could deny his ability to go out with these so-called "friends." You could ground him to the house on Friday and Saturday nights. And you could take away his keys and not let him drive.

Those are your three options. You could try to scare out of him his desire to be liked, to have friends, and to have a good time. Or, secondly, you could try to deny the validity of those desires. Or, third, you could try to regulate those desires out him. One or more of the options may work...for some kids...for awhile. But all three options suffer from the same fatal problem—they seek to suppress the teenager's desires rather than supplant them. They will ultimately fail because all three will leave your son's desires woefully unfulfilled.

And these three approaches are not just taken by countless parents towards wayward sons, but all of us are tempted to employ them in our everyday lives. You tend towards gluttony, so what do you do? You try to exercise self-control and deny yourself pleasure in eating. You are addicted to drugs, so you try, as Nancy Reagan taught us, to just say no. You are addicted to gambling, so you try to stop frequenting the casino and the gambling websites. And we all do so utilizing one of these three approaches, or all of them in combination. We try scaring the desire out of us by contemplating it's dangerous consequences. Or we try to deny the legitimacy of the desires at all as we pursue a life of self-denial for self-denial's sake alone. Or we seek to restrain our desires in a straight jacket of legalism.

But the problem is that all three approaches merely seek to restrain the wolf, not replace it. It is like trying to scare a wolf from eating sheep by warning it that the sheep herder will hunt him down and kill him should he do so. Or trying to tell the wolf that his desire for sheep is unnatural, a sin, a vice, and that virtuous wolfs do not desire sheep. Or you could to create so many hurdles and road blocks to the wolf's desires by fences, gates, moats, and electricity that the wolf may actually think that all these outward restraints have changed his heart. But the problem with all three approaches is that as soon as you let the wolf into the sheep pen it will kill one or more of the sheep. You haven't changed his heart, you have only caged it. A wolf in sheep's clothing, after all, is still a wolf.

And the same is true of the human heart. The human heart is a desire factory. No one sins out of duty. When

3

was the last time you woke up and said to yourself that you didn't want to sin that day but that you were going to do it anyway out of duty? When was the last time you lied, for instance, out of duty? You really didn't want to and otherwise won't have, but you did so out of duty? It is a rather confident assumption that this has not only never happened to you, but it has never happened to anyone ever in human history.

The reason people sin is because they want to. They believe the lie of sin—that by committing the sin they will be happier. That it will give them greater joy. Greater happiness. We were created to worship God. But as rebellious sinners, we instead worship ourselves. Unless and until we are birthed from above by the Holy Spirit into new creations, we seek to maximize our pleasure, happiness, and joy in the pursuit of romance, careers, popularity, power, money, and entertainment rather than God.

In Genesis, chapter 3, we read:

> [1] And the serpent has been subtile above every beast of the field which Yahweh God has made, and he says to the woman, "Is it true that God has said, "Do not eat of every tree of the garden?"'
>
> [2] And the woman says to the serpent, "Of the fruit of the trees of the garden we do eat, [3] and of the fruit of the tree which is in the midst of the garden God has said, 'Do not eat of it, nor touch it, lest you die.'"
>
> [4] And the serpent says to the woman, "Dying, you do not die. [5] For God knows that in the day of your eating of it—your

4

eyes have been opened, and you have been as God, knowing good and evil."

6 And the woman sees that the tree is good for food, and that it is pleasant to the eyes, and the tree is desirable to make one wise, and she takes of its fruit and eats, and gives also to her husband with her and he eats.

7 And the eyes of them both are opened, and they know that they are naked and they sew fig-leaves and make for themselves loin-coverings.   8 And they hear the sound of Yahweh God walking up and down in the garden at the breeze of the day, and the man and his wife hide themselves from the face of Yahweh God in the midst of the trees of the garden.

(Gen. 3:1-8 NYLT)

What is the essence of Adam and Eve's sin here? Was it the eating of the apple that got them kicked out of the Garden?   No!   Eating the apple was merely the outward manifestation of the sin they had already committed.   Chewing isn't sinful.   It may be the outward manifestation of the sin of gluttony.   Or the outward manifestation of the sin of eating poison to commit suicide. But chewing and eating are not, in and of themselves, the essence of sin.   Kissing, for instance, may be an outward manifestation of love, but it is not love.   So too, here, eating of the forbidden fruit, while wrong, was not the essence of evil.

Rather, in verse 6 we find three reasons why our first parents sinned:

1) They saw that the tree was good for food;
2) That it was pleasant to the eyes; and
3) Desirable to make one wise.

This is the essence of evil. This is the sin that our first parents committed that plunged all of humanity into total depravity. This is the sin that got them expelled from the Garden and placed them and their progeny under the sentence of eternal death. According to verse 6, the essence of evil is desiring something as more *good*, *desirable*, and *pleasant* than God. The essence of evil, then, is failing to find one's complete satisfaction in God supremely. The essence of evil is finding one's pleasure in the worship of one's self rather than in the worship of God.

We see this definition of sin further elaborated by God in the prophet Jeremiah:

> [11] "Has a nation changed gods? (And they are no gods!) But My people has changed their Glory for that which does not profit. [12] Be astonished, you heavens, at this! Yes, be frightened! Be greatly wasted!," affirms Yahweh. [13] "For My people has done two evils: they have forsaken Me, the fountain of living waters, to hew out for themselves wells—broken wells that contain no waters."
>
> (Jer. 2:11-13 NYLT)

In this passage God defines sin by forsaking Him, the only fount of living water, in order to dig for ourselves broken cisterns that, in the long run, hold no water. They are mirages. Or, to put it another way, the essence of evil is to sell oneself short of lasting happiness. To deny oneself eternal joy. The problem is not that we desire too much, but that we as sinful, rebellious creatures desire too little. We do not desire enough but fall short of pleasure without end. Sin is denying ourselves what will make us truly, fully, and eternally happy.

C.S. Lewis, a famous Christian apologist of the last century, wrote the following in a sermon entitled *The Weight of Glory*:

> If we consider the unblushing promises of reward and the staggering nature of the rewards promised in the Gospels, it would seem that our Lord finds our desires not too strong, but too weak. We are half-hearted creatures, fooling about with drink and sex and ambition when infinite joy is offered us, like an ignorant child who wants to go on making mud pies in a slum because he cannot imagine what is meant by the offer of a holiday at the sea. We are far too easily pleased.

"We are far too easily pleased." That is the essence of sin. We are too easily pleased, too easily satisfied, too easily content with the mud pies of this world, the empty cisterns of sin, the fleeting pleasures of rebellion. We live in a matrix weaved by the broken promises of sin and are blinded to the beauty to be had in God. We sin because we believe it's lie—that it, rather than God, will bring us the greater pleasure, and in doing so we are actually reaping eternal hell. We play with mud, and decay, and rot in shadows and darkness when infinite joy in blazing daylight is freely offered to us. That is the essence of evil.

Faith, therefore, if it is to save, must come out of the shadows and darkness and embrace infinite joy in the blazing daylight of God. We must not starve our desires for pleasure and happiness but rather indulge them fully. In order to be saved, we must become gluttons on the beauties and delights of God. As we are exhorted in the Song of Solomon, "Eat, friends, drink, and be drunk with love!" (Songs 5:1 ESV). Christianity is not a "do not" religion. It is not one of legalism. Rather, it is one in which believers are drunk on the love of God. Blaise Pascal reminds us that, "All men seek happiness," and therefore the Christian seeks to more truly, fully, and eternally satisfy that happiness in God rather than in mud pies.

Or as Thomas Chalmers put it, our desire to sin has been broken by "the explosive power of a new affection." We don't simply say "no" to sin. Rather, by rejecting our sinful desires as too pathetically small and shortsighted, we replace them with greater and higher affections for only that which will fill us with joy unspeakable and full of glory (1 Pet 1:8). We do not have to choose between happiness and obedience; rather, we maximize our joy in doing God's will.

Expositional Basis. You are probably thinking right now, "That sounds good and all, but how in the world did you get that out of our text from John 1:12-13? I don't see anything about mud pies or sin or joy in these verses at all. Help me see what you see!" So let's turn now to Scripture, and the Gospel of John in particular, to exegete how it defines saving faith as one that comes to Christ to receive

Him as one's treasure. That delights in Him. That worships Him.

I. John 1:10-13. First, it must be noted that the Apostle John never uses the noun *faith* in his Gospel. Rather, ninety-eight times he uses the verb *believe*. Ninety-eight! Why? Why does he always use the verb *believe* rather than the noun *faith*? One reason is to stress the verb nature of faith. Faith is not a one-time decision, commitment, prayer, or other act of the will. Rather, John always uses *believe* in the present-tense. So, for example, a more literal translation of John 3:16, probably the most famous verse in the Bible, reads, "For God so loved the world that He gave His only begotten Son, that whosoever is believing in Him should not perish but have eternal life." Saving faith is never past-tense. It is never completed. It is never a one-time deal. Rather, it is always continuous, ongoing, present-tense or else it was never saving faith to begin with.

But another reason that the Apostle John uses the verb *believe* rather than the noun *faith* is to emphasis the affectionate nature or essence of saving faith. Look with me again at our passage in John, chapter 1:

> 10 He was in the world, and the world was made through Him, and the world *did not know Him.* 11 To His own He came, and His own *did not receive Him.* 12 But as many *as did receive Him*, to them He gave authority to become sons of God, to those *believing in His name*: 13 who were begotten, not of bloods, nor of the will of flesh, nor of the will of man, but of God.

(Jn. 1:10-13 NYLT; emphasis added)

Look at the terms used by John for faith in this one passage alone. He describes unbelief in verse 10 as not knowing Christ, and in verse 11 as not receiving Him. Then, in contrast, in verse 12 he describes faith as both receiving Christ and believing in Him. So to summarize from this passage, saving faith is:

- **Verse 10:** Knowing Christ (see also Jn. 17:3).
- **Verse 11 & 12:** Receiving Christ.
- **Verse 12:** Believing in Christ.

Believing in Christ, therefore, is a knowing and receiving of Christ. Notice also that the Apostle uses the phrase in verse 12, "those who are believing *in* His name." Not only does John never use the word *faith* in his Gospel, but he also always gives the object of a Christian's believing—*in* Christ. Not believing about Christ. Not having a head full of knowledge about Christ. But to be ongoing, continuously, present-tense believing *in* the Person and work of Christ.

It is essential to know certain things about Christ before one can exercise saving faith.[1] But dead orthodoxy never saved anyone. Just look at the devil. Jacob, the half-brother of Christ, tells us that Satan has a more pristine theology that any human who has ever lived, and yet it avails him not (Jac. 2:19). Or as Jesus condemned the religious leaders of His day in Matthew 15:

---

[1] For a more indepth exegesis of the *notitia*—or knowledge—component of saving faith, please see Chapter 4, pages 85- 91, of my book *The Five Solas: An Expository Exhortation.*

7 "Hypocrites, well did Isaiah prophesy of you, saying:

8 'This people draw near to Me with their mouth,

And with their lips honor Me,

But their heart is far off from Me.

9 And in vain do they worship Me,

Teaching the commands of men as teachings.'"

(Matt. 15:7-9 NYLT)

The purpose of the Church, goal of the Christian walk, is theology as doxology producing holiness. Or, to put it another way, doctrine as worship producing love. Doctrine and praise are two sides of the same coin and should naturally lead to perfecting holiness before the Lord (2 Cor. 7:1). As Shai Linne put it in his song *Doxology Intro*:

> Theology is the study of God and it's very important;
> Doxology is an expression of praise to God.
> So, the point here is that all theology should ultimately lead to doxology.
> If theology doesn't lead to doxology, then we've actually missed the point of theology.
> So if you have theology without doxology, you just have dead, cold orthodoxy;
> Which is horrible, right?
> On the other side, we have people who say: "Ugh! Forget theology; I just wanna praise!" Right?

> But, if we have doxology without theology,
> we actually have idolatry!
> Because it's just a random expression of
> praise; but it's not actually informed by the
> Truth of who God is.
> So, God is concerned with both!
> He's concerned with an accurate
> understanding of Him;
> And that accurate understanding of Him,
> leading to a response of praise, adoration
> and worship towards Him.

We must have theology. We must have doctrine. We must have an accurate understanding of God. But if this theology, doctrine, and accurate understanding of God does not lead to praise and worship, adoration and exultation, it is meaningless. The study of God should be done as the worship of God which results in the fruits of love and obedience. Therefore, saving faith does not merely believe in a doctrine called Jesus, no matter how pristine it is, but rather must joyfully embrace, or receive, the Person of Christ.

II. Other uses in John. So just from John 1:10-13 we have seen that the Apostle John describes saving faith as a knowing, receiving, and believing in Christ. Next, let us look at other terms the Apostle uses to describe saving faith in the remainder of his Gospel.

II.A. Thirst. In John, chapter 4, we read:

> [7] There comes a woman out of Samaria to
> draw water. Jesus says to her, "Give me to

drink." [8] For His disciples were gone away to the city that they may buy food.

[9] Therefore the Samaritan woman says to Him, "How do You, being a Jew, ask a drink from me, being a Samaritan woman?" For Jews have no dealing with Samaritans.

[10] Jesus answered and said to her, "If you had known the gift of God, and who it is who is saying to you, 'Give Me a drink," you would have asked Him, and He would have given you living water."

[11] The woman says to Him, "Lord, You do not even have a vessel to draw with, and the well is deep. Where, then, do You the have living water? [12] Are You greater than our father Jacob, who gave us the well, and did drink out of it himself, and his sons and his cattle?"

[13] Jesus answered and said to her, "Everyone who is drinking of this water shall thirst again, [14] but whoever may drink of the water that I will give him may not thirst—to the age. But the water that I will give him shall become in him a well of water springing up to life age-enduring."

(Jn. 4:7-14 NYLT)

In this passage Jesus describes Himself as living water (vs. 10) that "shall become in [a believer] a well of water springing up to life age-enduring" (vs. 14). And here Jesus describes saving faith as thirsting and coming to

Christ to drink from Him (vs. 13-14). We see this confirmed a few chapters later in John, chapter 7:

> [37] And in the last day, the great day of the feast, Jesus stood and cried, saying, "If anyone thirsts, let him come to Me and drink! [38] He who is believing in Me, according as the Holy Writing has said, out of his belly shall flow rivers of living water!"
>
> (Jn. 7:37-38 NYLT)

"'If anyone thirsts, let him come to Me and drink!'" (vs. 37). That is the essence of saving faith. As we just saw, everyone thirsts. Everyone seeks their own pleasure. Their own happiness. Their own joy. God designed the human heart to thirst. And here Jesus cries out to a lost and dying world—not to scare, deny, or regulate away their desires—but to rather more truly, fully, and eternally satisfy those desires in Him. Saving faith, therefore, does not merely consist of *knowledge*, *assent* (i.e., agreement), and *trust.*, but of a *thirsting* and *drinking* of the Person of Christ.

II.B. Hunger. In the 6th chapter 6 of John, Jesus tells us that: "'I am the bread of life. He who comes to Me shall never hunger, and he who believes in Me shall never thirst.'" And then again in verse 48: "'I am the bread of life.'" And again in verse 51: "'I am the living bread which came down from heaven. If anyone eats of this bread, he will live forever.'"

Jesus uses five verbs interchangeably to describe saving faith in this passage: *coming* (vs. 35), *hungering* (vs. 35), *believing* (vs. 35), *thirsting* (vs. 35), and *eating* (vs. 51). Saving faith, therefore, is not reciting a prayer, signing a card, or walking the aisle to the altar. Rather, saving faith is an affectionate desire for Christ. A desperate longing to satisfy the deepest longings of one's soul in Christ. Once, again, therefore, we see that saving faith does not merely consist of *knowledge*, *assent* (i.e., agreement), and *trust.*, but in the *coming*, *hunger*, *believing*, *thirsting*, and *eating* of the Person of Christ.

II.C.   Love.   The final stop in our journey through the Gospel of John begins with the third chapter:

> 18 "He who is believing in Him is not judged, but he who is not believing has been judged already, because he has not believed in the name of the only begotten Son of God. 19 And this is the judgment, that the light has come to the world, and men did love the darkness rather than the light, for their works were evil. 20 For everyone who is doing wicked things hates the light, and does not come to the light, that his works may not be convicted.
>
> (Jn. 3:18-20 NYLT)

In order to see how saving faith is defined in this passage, it is necessary to first look at how Jesus describes those without saving faith:

- **Verse 18:** Not believing.
- **Verse 19:** Loving darkness.
- **Verse 20:** Hating the light.

So if those who do not having saving faith are not believing, loving darkness, and hating the light, then those with saving faith must, of necessity, have the opposite affections. They must be believing (vs. 18). They must be loving the light (vs. 19). They must be hating the darkness (vs. 20). Believing, loving the light, and hating sin are all used here by Jesus interchangeably to describe saving faith. You cannot have one without the other, or you are a liar who has deceived himself. Once again, therefore, we see that saving faith does not merely consist of *knowledge*, *assent* (i.e., agreement), and *trust.*, but in *believing*, *loving the light*, and *hating the darkness*.

We see this confirmed several chapters later in John:

> [41] "I do not receive glory from man. [42] But I have known you, that the agape of God you have not in yourselves. [43] I have come in the name of My Father, and you do not receive Me; if another may come in his own name, him you will receive. [44] How are you able to believe, who are receiving glory from one another, and you do not seek the glory that is from the only God?"
>
> (Jn. 5:41-44 NYLT)

Here Jesus uses four terms to describe unbelievers:

- **Verse 42:** They do not have the love of God in them.
- **Verse 43:** They do not receive Him.
- **Verse 44:** They do not believe Him.
- **Verse 44:** They do not seek glory that comes from God.

Again, if those who do not having saving faith are not loving God, receiving Christ, believing in Christ, and seeking glory from God rather than men, then those with saving faith must, of necessity, have the opposite affections. They must have the love of God in them (vs. 42). They must receive Christ (vs. 43). They must be believing in Him (vs. 44). They must be seeking the honor that only comes from God (vs. 44). Once, again, therefore, we see that saving faith does not merely consist of *knowledge*, *assent* (i.e., agreement), and *trust.*, but in *loving, receiving, believing*, and *seeking honor from God*.

And we see this love component of saving faith reflected in Jesus' High Priestly Prayer found in John 17, where in verse 26 He states, "'And I have declared to them Your name, and will declare it, that the love with which You loved Me may be in them, and I in them.'" You cannot, therefore, having saving faith without loving Christ. It is a spiritual impossibility.

To summarize, in the Gospel of John we have seen saving faith described as:

• Knowing, receiving, and believing in the Person of Christ;

• Thirsting for and drinking of the Person of Christ;

• Coming, hunger, believing, thirsting, and eating of the Person of Christ;

• Loving the light (i.e., the Person of Christ (Jn. 1:4)) and hating sin;

• Having the love of God for Christ, receiving Christ, believing in Him, and seeking glory from God alone.

III. Other uses in the rest of the New Testament. We have finished examining out how saving faith is described in the Gospel of John, but now we must also consider how it is depicted in the rest of Scripture as well. To make it easier to understand, I will attempt to classifying these descriptions by category.

III.A. Tasting. First, saving faith is depicted as a coming and tasting of the pleasures of God. We just saw several passages in the Gospel of John where saving faith is described as thirsting and drinking of the Person of Christ (Jn. 4:14, 7:37-38) and hungering and feasting upon the Person of Christ (Jn. 6:35, 51). And we see this confirmed elsewhere in Scripture. For instance, the Apostle John writes in Revelation 22:17:

> And the Spirit and the bride say, "Come!" And he who is hearing, let him say, "Come!" And he who is thirsting, let him come! And he who is willing, let him take the water of life freely!
>
> (Rev. 22:17 NYLT)

Here again faith is described as a *coming*, *thirsting*, and *drinking*—"let him who thirsts come and take the water of life freely!" In 1 Peter, chapter 2, we read:

> [1] Having put aside, then, all evil, and all deceit, and hypocrisies, and envyings, and all evil speakings, [2] as new-born babes long for the pure milk that in it you may grow, [3] if indeed you did taste that the Lord is gracious.

18

(1 Pet. 2:1-3 NYLT)

Saving faith is receiving—a tasting—of Christ as completely satisfying. Or as the psalmist tells us, it is "tasting and seeing that Yahweh is good" (Ps. 34:8). Or as the author of Hebrews puts it, "tast[ing] the good word of God" (Heb. 6:5).

III.B. Supreme Treasure. Secondly, saving faith is described as treasuring the Person of Christ. We see this in Matthew, chapter 13:

> [44] "Again, the kingdom of the heavens is like treasure hidden in the field, which a man having found hide, and from his joy goes and sells all—as much as he has—and buys that field.
> [45] "Again, the kingdom of the heavens is like to a man, a merchant, seeking good pearls, [46] who, having found one pearl of great price, having gone away, has sold all—as much as he had—and bought it.
>
> (Matt. 13:44-46 NYLT)

Saving faith, therefore, seizes upon Christ as supremely valuable. At the moment of conversion, a born-again man sees Christ as a hidden treasure, a pearl of unfathomable worth, (2 Cor. 4:4, 6) for whom he joyfully renounces all his worldly treasures to obtain. We see this in the testimony of the Apostle Paul in Philippians 3:

> [7] But what things were to me gains, these I have counted, because of Messiah, loss.
> [8] Yes, indeed, and I count all things to be

> loss, because of the excellency of the knowledge of Messiah Jesus my Lord, because of whom I suffered the loss of all things, and do count them to be dung, that I may gain Messiah, 9 and be found in Him, not having my own righteousness, which is of the law, but that which is through faith in Christ—the righteousness that is from God by faith.
>
> (Phil. 3:7-9 NYLT)

At the moment of conversion, a born-again man sees everything he once held dear as rubbish compared to Christ. His treasure, like Paul's, is now to gain Christ and be found in Him. Or as Peter put it, "Therefore, to you who believe He is precious" (1 Pet. 2:7). Or as Paul put it, Christ is our treasure in jars of clay (2 Cor. 4:7).

In Hebrews, chapter 11, we read:

> 4 By faith Moses, having become great, refused to be called a son of the daughter of Pharaoh, 25 having chosen rather to be afflicted with the people of God than to have sin's pleasure for a season,26 having reckoned the reproach of the Messiah greater wealth than the treasures in Egypt, for he was fixed upon the recompense of reward.
>
> (Heb. 11:24-26 NYLT)

Saving faith is described here in verse 26 as valuing Christ as the greatest of all riches. Greater than all the riches of Egypt, or of the entire world for that matter. Greater than, as verse 25 tells us, the fleeting pleasures of sin. Saving faith, verse 26 tells us, treasures Christ as an infinitely glorious reward.

Saving faith, therefore, treasures Christ, prizes Christ, and values Christ supremely. Saving faith occurs when He becomes more precious to you than anything that life has to offer or that death can take away. He becomes your magnificent obsession. He becomes, as God promised Abraham, your "exceedingly great reward" (Gen. 15:1).

IIi.C. Supreme Love. Third, saving faith is also described as loving God. We see this in 1 Corinthians, chapter 16:

> If anyone does not brotherly love the Lord Jesus Messiah, let him be anathema! Maranatha—O Lord come!
> (1 Cor. 16:22 NYLT)

The Apostle Paul cannot be more clearer that the main element of saving faith is love than he is here: if you do not love Christ, you have never had saving faith and are damned. This echoes what we had seen earlier in John 3:18-20 and 5:41-44.

Similarly, in 2 Thessalonians, chapter 2, the Apostle Paul describes what will happen to non-believers:

> 9 whose presence is according to the working of the Adversary, in all power, and signs, and lying wonders, 10 and in all unrighteous deceitfulness in those perishing, because they did not receive the love of the truth for their being saved.
> (2 Thess. 2:9-10 NYLT)

Here again we see that those who do not believe are described as those who do not receive the love of the truth. So to believe in Christ is to love the truth. And as Jesus Himself tells us, He alone is the way, the truth, and the life (Jn. 14:6). So, once more, we see that to believe in Christ is to love Christ, and to not believe in Christ is not to love Christ. Saving faith, therefore, is love for Christ.

Finally, in 2 Timothy, chapter 4, we read:

> 7 The good strife I have striven, the course I have finished, the faith I have kept. 8 Henceforth, there is laid up for me the crown of the righteousness that the Lord, the Righteous Judge, shall render to me in that day, and not only to me, but also to all those loving His appearing.
>
> (2 Tim. 4:7-8 NYLT)

Saving faith, therefore, is to lovingly long for the consummation of Christ's glorious and triumphant reign over creation (see also Matt. 24:42, 44, 25:13; Mk. 13:35; 1 Thess. 1:10, 5:6; Tit. 2:13; Heb. 9:28; Rev. 16:15). It is lovingly longing for HIm to be worshipped by the whole earth. it is loving longing for His imminent appearing, even if His return means never finishing your home remolding, or the dream vacation you have planned for next year, or retiring and enjoying your golden years, or marrying your sweetheart. Out of love for Christ, His triumphant return is much more precious than anything you desire upon this earth.

III.D. Supreme Enjoyment. Fourth and finally, saving faith is also depicted as receiving Christ as one's supreme enjoyment. As one's supreme pleasure. As one's supreme joy. We read earlier in 2 Thessalonians of the Apostle Paul's description of the unbelievers as those who do not obey the truth. But in the very next verse, he describes them as those who "had pleasure in unrighteousness" (2:11). Conversely, therefore, if those without saving faith have pleasure in unrighteousness, those with saving faith have pleasure in righteousness. They seek to satisfy their pleasure in that fount of everlasting righteousness—Jesus Christ.

We see this, for instance, in Psalm 16:

> You cause me to know the path of life;
> Fulness of joys is in Your presence;
> At Your right hand are pleasures
> forevermore!
>
> (Ps. 16:11 NYLT)

"Fulness of joys is in Your presence; at Your right hand are pleasures forevermore!" Notice the adjectives *fulness* and *forevermore*. If someone came up to you and offered you only a single lifetime of happiness, joy, and pleasure, you would be a fool to take it. And yet that is the lie that sin promises us hour after hour, day after day, and the lie that every single human is prone to believe. By both nature and choice, we willingly crave the 80 years of pleasure in this life at the expense of eternal fulness of joy and pleasures forevermore. But the gift of saving faith shows us how blind we've been and reveals to us the source of true and lasting joy.

Then look a few pages over to Psalm 21:

> For You make him blessings forever;
> You have made him joyful with gladness in
> Your presence.

(Ps. 21:6 NYLT)

Again, in Psalm, chapter 43, we read:

> And I go to the altar of God,
> To God—the gladness of my joy;
> And I thank You with a harp,
> O God, my God.
>
> (Ps. 43:4 NYLT)

Here again we see that saving faith is when God is the gladness of your joy. Echoing this, we read in 1 Peter 1:

> whom, not having seen, you agape. In whom, though now not seeing, you are believing as you rejoice with joy inexpressible and glorified,
>
> (1 Pet. 1:8 NYLT)

Notice that Peter not only describes saving faith in this verse as loving Christ and believing in Christ, but also as a rejoicing in Christ "with joy unspeakable and glorified." Finally, in John, chapter 15, we find:

> "These things I have spoken to you, that My joy may remain in you and your joy may be full."
>
> (Jn. 15:11 NYLT)

Our union with Christ is the fulness of Christ's joy abiding in us. Saving faith, therefore, is feasting upon the joy that a born-again man now has in God's presence. It is the delight he has in the eternal pleasures that he now enjoys at God's right hand. It is an insatiable but always satisfying desire for God as the source of joy unspeakable and full of glory.

And this joy leads to peace. Again, as Jesus told His disciples the night before His crucifixion:

> "Peace I leave to you. My peace I give to you; not according as the world gives do I give to you. Let not your heart be troubled, nor let it be afraid."
> (Jn. 14:27 NYLT)

Or as He told them a little later in the evening of Maundy Thursday:

> "These things I have spoken to you, that in me you may have peace. In the world you shall have tribulation, but take courage—I have overcome the world."
> (Jn. 16:33 NYLT)

Or as the Apostle Paul calls it in Philippians, "the peace of God which surpasses all understanding that will guard our hearts and minds through Christ Jesus" (Phil. 4:7). In short, the one with saving faith is blessed. The Greek word for *blessed* is *makarios*, which the Greeks used in reference to their gods. They called them "the blessed ones" because they had achieved a state of happiness and contentment that was beyond the cares, stress, worry, and problems of earth. But in the Beatitudes, Jesus uses the term to describe the state of His believers (Matt. 5:3-10; Lk. 6:20-23). Saving faith, therefore, is joy in Christ that leads to peace in Christ that is not dependent on external circumstances but upon one's being hidden in Christ (Col. 3:3).

So, **to summarize**, from the rest of Scripture we have seen saving faith described as coming and tasting of the Person of Christ, loving the Person of Christ, treasuring the Person of Christ, and enjoyment of the Person of Christ. It is the falling out of love with ourselves and the idols of our hearts and falling in love with God.

Concluding Implications:

In conclusion, therefore, saving faith is coming to, receiving, tasting, and seeing the irresistible beauties of Christ. Saving faith is an act of affectionate worship. And this cannot be manufactured or produced by fallen, depraved humanity, but rather has to be effectually wrought in the heart at the moment of regeneration by the Holy Spirit in order for sinful man to find Christ beautiful. We need new eyes of the heart in order to see Christ as beautiful. And this is what the Apostle Paul tells us happens at the moment of new birth:

> [3] But if also our gospel is veiled, it is veiled in those perishing— [4] in whom the god of this age did blind the minds of the unbelieving—that there does not shine forth to them the enlightening of the gospel of the glory of the Messiah, who is the image of God. [5] For we do not herald ourselves, but Messiah Jesus as Lord, and ourselves as your slaves because of Jesus. [6] Because it is God who said, "Out of darkness light is to shine," who did shine in our hearts for the enlightening of

the knowledge of the glory of God in the
face of Jesus Messiah.

(2 Cor. 4:3-6 NYLT)

Here the Apostle describes conversion in two ways:

• **Verse 4:**   The light of the gospel of the glory of
Christ, who is the image of God.
• **Verse 6:**   The light of the knowledge of the glory of
God in the face of Jesus Christ.

Verses 3-4 tell us, however, that "the god of this
age" (i.e., Satan), has blinded and veiled the eyes of
nonbelievers lest the light of the Gospel should shine on
them. But verse 6 tells us that, just as God spoke light into
existence at the moment of creation, so at the moment of
conversion He speaks the light of His gospel into the heart
of a regenerated man.

Therefore, you must ask yourself if God has indeed
spoken the light of His gospel into your heart in which you
find Christ irresistibly beautiful.   Ask yourself if you have
this saving faith—in which you are receiving, coming to,
treasuring, loving, and enjoying Christ—by asking yourself
the following questions:

1.   Is Christ more precious to you than anything life
has to offer or death can take away?
2.   Does your soul thirst for the living God (Ps. 42:2)
by panting after communion with Him through prayer
and the prayerful meditation of HIs Word. When a guy
meets a girl and love blossoms between them, they
can't help but spend time together. Is it that way with
you and God?

3. Are you unable to find contentment in anything without God? Or are you content with the mud pies of this world? Are you content to find your happiness in the fleeting pleasures of this life? Just as a man in love with a woman is not content to tolerate any substitute, so a believer is not content with anything other than God. Even all the splendors and riches of heaven itself, without God, would be hell for a believer.

4. Do you hate that which separates you from God (i.e., sin)? Loath it? Despise it? Flee from it? Or do you tolerate it and enjoy it? Do you find sin attractive? Do you laugh and applaud the sin of others that God hates?

5. Do you praise God out of the overflow of worship and delight for Him? And do you seek to draw others from among your unbelieving friends, family, neighbors, and co-workers into the delight and adulation of Christ? Do you seek to do everything for the glory of God?

6. Finally, are you willing to forsake all, suffer all, endure all, and obey all in obedient service to the Lover of your soul? Is Christ worth more to you than any sinful delight this world has to offer? Is He worth more than all the persecution and ridicule the world might hurl at you? Is He worth dying for?

If you have been convicted that you do not have this saving faith, then I plead with you to beg God to create this faith in you. For Jesus tell us that this is eternal life—that we may experimentally know God the Father, the only true God, and Jesus Christ His Son (Jn. 17:3).

And in another place Jesus tells us that only those who seek with a desperate forcefulness to enter the Kingdom of God will do so (Matt. 11:12; Lk. 16:16).

Therefore, ask, and keep on asking; seek, and keep on seeking; knock, and keep on knocking (Matt. 7:7-11; Lk. 11:5-13) until you know that you are a child of God. Cry out to God all night if you have to until He births you into a new creation! Do not keep silent and give Him no rest (Isaiah 62:1, 6-7; 18:1-8) until you know beyond a shadow of doubt that you have been born of the Spirit with a new heart and a new nature! Do not go to bed tonight until you know with unmistakeable certainty that your sins have been forgiven and that you are reconciled and at peace with God! The fate of your eternal soul hangs in the balance.

NATHAN W. TUCKER

2 THE ESSENCE OF SAVING FAITH IS LOVE

I. *T*he Necessary Overflow of God's Joy. This week we are going to look at the necessity of saving faith as the overflow of the fact that God is love. Because God exists as a Trinity, saving faith must, of necessity, partake of the overflow of joy that the Triune God has in and of Himself. Saving faith joins in God's eternal triune love. Saving faith participates in God's infinite joy in being God. Saving faith reciprocates God's delight in being God. Saving faith receives and overflows with God's love as it is poured out into our hearts by the Holy Spirit (Rom. 5:5).

I.A. God is Love. In order to understand this, we first must climb the very heights of the Himalayas of Scriptural insight and peer into what may be known and deduced of the relationship of the Triune Godhead. And the key to beginning to understand this great mystery is the fact, as the Apostle John tells us, that "God is love" (1 Jn. 4:8, 16).

If you believe in a divine being, you probably have no problem agreeing with this statement. But what people mean when they say that God is love is not what the Bible means by saying that God is love. When an unregenerate pagan says that God is love, what they really mean is that God is love to the exclusion of all His other attributes. They mean that God is love, but not just, angry, or wrathful, and thereby they not only deny the entire testimony of Scripture but the personality of God as well. And too often they equate love with God, as if love and God are identical, equal, and interchangeable. But by making an emotion God, then we are all under obligation to worship love as God, which is not only nonsensical but blasphemous.

31

However, when Scripture says that God is love, it simply means that love is an essential aspect of God's character, not His complete character. "God is love" simply sums up the entire Scriptural record of who God is. And the rest of that Biblical witness to God helps us define what His love is. As the twentieth century pastor and theologian A.W. Tozer wrote in his book *The Knowledge of the Holy*:

> We can know, for instance, that because God is self-existent, His love has no beginning; because He is eternal, His love can have no end; because He is infinite, it has no limit; because He is holy, it is the quintessence of all spotless purity; because He is immense, His love is an incomprehensible, vast, bottomless, shoreless sea before which we kneel in joyful silence and from which the loftiest eloquence retreats confused and abashed.

I.B. Love Requires the Trinity. But by saying that God is love, we have a dilemma. For the Bible declares that God is the Great I Am—the uncreated, self-sufficient, self-existent, unchangeable, limitless One who has no beginning, no end, no need, and no weakness (Ex. 3:14-15; Numb. 23:19; Ps. 33:11, 102:27; Mal. 3:6; Jn. 5:26; Heb. 13:8; Jac. 1:17; Rev.1:8, 22:13). The problem we face, therefore, is how can a solitary god love if there is no one else to love?

As author Jared C. Wilson explains:

A solitary god cannot be love. He may learn to love. He may yearn for love. But he cannot in himself be love, since love requires an object. Real love requires relationship. In the doctrine of the Trinity we finally see how love is part of the fabric of creation; it's essential to the eternal, need-nothing Creator. From eternity past, the Father and the Son and the Spirit have been in community, in relationship. They have loved each other. That loving relationship is bound up in the very nature of God himself. If God were not a Trinity but merely a solitary divinity, he could neither be love nor be God.

Fred Sanders, in his book entitled *The Deep Things of God: How the Trinity Changes Everything*, wrote:

The doctrine of the Trinity expels a host of unworthy ideas about God's love. . . .God is not lonely, or bored, or selfish. . . . This is what the doctrine of the Trinity helps us learn with greater precision: that God is love. The triune God is a love that is infinitely high above you, eternally preceding you, and welcoming you in.

I.C. The Triune God as Love. Scripture defines the Triune God in this way: one God, eternally existent in three Persons—God the Father, God the Son, and God the Holy Spirit. These three Persons of the Godhead are equal in every perfection, and that these three are one God, having precisely the same nature, attributes, and perfections, and worthy of precisely the same homage, confidence, and obedience (Genesis 1; Leviticus 19:2; Deuteronomy 6:4-5; Isaiah 5:16; 6:1-7; 40:18-31; Matthew 3:16-17; 28:19-20; John 14:6-27; 1 Corinthians 8:6; 2 Corinthians 13:14; Galatians 4:4-6; Ephesians 2:13-18; 1 John 1:5; 4:8).

I.C.1.   God the Father is the Deity existing, as 18th century pastor and theologian Jonathan Edwards explains, "in the prime, unoriginated, and most absolute manner, or the Deity in its direct existence." This is why He is called the *Father*. He, for instance, begot the Son. He is the One whose will Jesus obeyed and whose words Jesus spoke during His earthly ministry.   He is the One who Jesus prayed to. He is the one who sends forth the Holy Spirit. God the Father is God in "the prime, unoriginated, and most absolute manner...the Deity in its direct existence."

I.C.2.   God the Son, as Edwards goes on to explain, "is the Deity generated by God's understanding of Himself, and subsisting in that idea."   God the Son is the self-expression of God the Father.   He is God the Father's understanding of Himself so perfectly so as to become a living reproduction, or begetting, of Himself as a distinct and separate Person. God the Son has eternally existed with God the Father as the Father's image or idea of Himself.

C.S. Lewis explains it this way in his book *Mere Christianity*:

He is always, so to speak, streaming forth from the Father, like light from a lamp...or thoughts from a mind. He is the self-expression of the Father—what the Father has to say. And there was never a time when He was not saying it.

It is impossible for us as finite creatures to perfectly know ourselves, so all analogies are going to be woefully inadequate. But let's imagine that the person staring back at you in the mirror suddenly popped out of the mirror and became a living, personal human being. He would not only look like you but act like you with your personality and character. He would be your double in every way; a perfect image of yourself.

Or, let's imagine that we were able to make a complete clone of you. Not only of your genetic DNA, but we were able to somehow map your personality and character, thought patterns and memories, and upload all of that into your clone. He would be an exact, perfect carbon copy of you, but yet a distinct and separate living, volitional, and emotional person.

These illustrations are probably the closest we as mere mortals can get to grasping God the Son as the mirror image of the Father. But, like all human analogies, they are imperfect. Their biggest flaw is their inability to illustrate the singular unity of God the Son as the same essence, nature, and substance of God the Father. There is one God, consisting of three separate and distinct Persons—a mystery for which we have no real analogy for. One substance, three Persons. Not personalities or modes, but Persons. One essence, but three living, volitional, and emotional Persons.

Perhaps the closest is a three-headed man—three brains, three consciousness, three personalities, three wills, but one physical property. We may call him Robert, but each head or Person we may call Bobby, Rob, and Roberto respectively. But this analogy loses the strengths of the first two—the shared personality and character, thought patterns and memories, of the individuals. So to better complete this analogy, each person in this three-headed man would be an identical clone—mentally, emotionally, intellectually—of the others, but yet be a distinct and separate Person.

But though these illustrations are imperfect, we see the idea they represent confirmed throughout the testimony of Scripture. For instance, the Apostle Paul describes Jesus as "the image of God" (2 Cor. 4:4) and "the image of the invisible God" (Col. 1:15). The author of Hebrews describes God the Son as "the radiance of God's glory and the exact representation of His substance, sustaining all things by His powerful word" (Heb. 1:3; see also 2 Cor. 4:6). Though Christ was, "in the nature of God, [He] did not consider His equality with God to be grasped" (Phil. 2:6). Finally, as Jesus Himself declared, "'Anyone who has seen Me has seen the Father'" (Jn. 14:9).

And there was never a time before the Father begot or reproduced the Son. Nor could there be for the simple reason that God is eternally perfect. Therefore He has always had a perfect understanding of Himself eternally projected as the living and infinite God the Son. It is impossible for this Word, or image, or imprint, or thought of the Father to be even a fraction of a nanosecond less eternal than the Father Himself. You cannot have one without the other. Again, therefore, it must be stressed that using the term *begetting* simply describes relations of origin within the Godhead and not degrees of subordination or inferiority.

In short, Scripture teaches that from eternity past the eternal Father has always had:

• A perfect image of Himself (2 Cor. 4:4; Col. 1:15, 4:4).

• A perfect reflection or radiance of His glory (2 Core. 4:6; Heb. 1:3).

• A perfect nature of His essence (Phil. 2:6)

• A perfect form of His Person (Jn. 14:9)

And this perfect image, reflection, nature, and form is God the Son. As pastor and theologian John Piper put it:

> Since the Son is the image of God and the reflection of God and the stamp of God and the form of God, equal with God, and indeed is God, therefore God's delight in the Son is delight in Himself. Therefore, the original, the primal, the deepest, the foundational joy of God is the joy He has in His own perfections as He sees them reflected in His Son. He loves the Son and delights in the Son and takes pleasure in the Son because the Son is God Himself.

We see this in Matthew, chapter 17:

> [1] And after six days Jesus takes Peter, Jacob, and John his brother, and brings them up to a high mountain by themselves, [2] and He was transfigured

before them: His face shone as the sun and His garments did become white as the light. 3 And behold!—Moses and Elijah did appear to them, talking together with Him.

4 And Peter answering said to Jesus, "Lord, it is good to us to be here. If You will, we may make here three tents: for You one, and for Moses one, and one for Elijah."

5 While he is yet speaking, behold!—a bright cloud overshadowed them, and behold!—a voice out of the cloud, saying, "This is My Son, the Agaped, in whom I did delight. Hear Him!"

6 And the disciples having heard, did fall upon their face, and were exceedingly afraid. 7 And Jesus, having come near, touched them and said, "Rise, be not afraid!" 8 And having lifted up their eyes, they saw no one except Jesus only.

(Matt. 17:1-8 NYLT)

There are three necessarily vital things to note in this passage. First, that God the Father gave these three Apostles a glimpse of Jesus' true glory as God the Son. We see this confirmed by Peter in the second chapter of his second epistle:

> For having received from God the Father honor and glory when such a voice being borne to Him by the Excellent Glory: "This is My Son, the agaped, in whom I was well pleased."

(2 Pet. 1:17 NYLT)

Look at what Peter says—that on the Mount of Transfiguration God the Father bestowed upon God the Son "honor and glory." John also makes reference to Christ's transfiguration when he states that the disciples, "beheld His glory, the glory as of the only begotten of the Father" (Jn. 1:14). Christ was revealed on the mountain to be fully God—of the same essence, nature, and equality.

The second thing to note is that God the Father called Jesus His agaped Son. In the Greek language, *agape* love is the highest form, the highest kind, of love. It is an unconditional, self-giving love. Jesus is God's beloved Son. And third and finally, it is important to note that God the Father states of Christ that He is delighted, or well pleased, in Him.

He says these two things—that Christ is His agaped Son and that He is well pleased in Him—on one other occasion: at Jesus' baptism as the Father anoints Him with the Holy Spirit (Matt. 3:7; Mk. 1:11; Lk. 3:22). Therefore, God the Father finds infinite pleasure, joy, delight, and happiness in God the Son as He loves, treasures, embraces, admires, and worships Christ. And the only way it is impossible for this to constitute idolatry is if God the Son is fully and equally God.

We see this confirmed in several other places as well. Jesus testifies that, "'The Father loves the Son, and has given all things into His hand'" (Jn. 3:35). Again, Jesus tells us, "'For the Father loves the Son, and shows Himself all things that He Himself does; and He will show Him greater works than these, that you may marvel'" (Jn. 5:20). Speaking through the prophet Isaiah, God declares of the coming Messiah, "'Behold!—My Servant whom I uphold; My Elect One in whom My soul delights!'" (Is. 42:1). Once again, therefore, we see that God the Father finds infinite pleasure, joy, delight, and happiness in God the Son as He loves, treasures, embraces, admires, and worships Christ as Himself.

And Christ, in turn, finds infinite pleasure, joy, delight, and happiness in God the Father as He loves, treasures, embraces, admires, and worships the prime, unoriginated, and most absolute Deity. For the Bible tells us that this God-man Jesus Christ, though being of the very nature and essence of God, did not come to earth to seize by force equality with God (Phil. 2:6). Rather, "He emptied Himself of His divine privileges, took the form of a slave, and was made in the likeness of men" (Phil. 2:7). In other words, though He was very God of very God, Jesus "did not live to please Himself" (Rom. 15:3), but rather became the submissive and obedient love-slave of His Father. He lovingly obeyed His Father's will by humbling Himself in becoming a Man.

He further lovingly obeyed His Father by submitting to His will, telling us that, "I have come down from heaven, not to do My own will but the will of Him who sent Me" (Jn. 8:38). So in love was He with His Father that He declared to His disciples that, "My food is to do the will of Him who sent Me and to finish His work" (Jn. 4:34). Elsewhere Jesus declared, "I can of Myself do nothing...I do not seek My own will, but the will of the Father who sent Me...I always do those things that please Him" (Jn. 5:30, 6:29). Out of loving obedience, the very words Jesus said (Jn. 12:49, 17:8) and the works He performed (Jn. 5:36) were dictated to Him by God the Father from eternity past. Finally, out of loving obedience, God the Son humbled

Himself to die as a propitiation for sins upon the cross of Calvary (Phil. 2:8).

God the Father and God the Son, therefore, have eternally had mutually infinite pleasure, joy, delight, and happiness in each other as They love, treasure, embrace, admire, and worship the mirror divine perfections They behold in one another.

I.C.3. This, in turn, helps us understand **God the Holy Spirit**. As Edwards explains, He is "the Deity subsisting in act, or the divine essence flowing out and breathed forth, in God's infinite love to and delight in Himself." In other words, the Holy Spirit is the love birthed out—or breathed out—of the mutual delight that has eternally existed between God the Father and God the Son. Again, the Holy Spirit was not created; He is no less eternal than the other two Persons of the Godhead. He has always existed as the Spirit of Love between the members of the Deity.

As C.S. Lewis goes on to explain in *Mere Christianity*:

> Much the most important thing to know [about the relationship between God the Father and God the Son] is that it is a relationship of love. The Father delights in the Son; the Son looks up to His Father....What the Christians mean by the statement "God is love" (1John 4:8) ... is that the living, dynamic activity of love has been going on in God forever and has created everything else....In Christianity God is not a static thing... but a dynamic, pulsating activity, a life, almost a kind of

drama. Almost, if you will not think me irreverent, a kind of dance.

The union between the Father and the Son is such a live concrete thing that this union itself is also a Person. I know this is almost inconceivable, but look at th[i]s. You know that among human beings, when they get together in a family, or a club, or a trade union, people talk about the "spirit" of that family, or club, or trade union. They talk about it's "spirit" because the individual members, when they are together, do really develop particular ways of talking and behaving which they would not have if they were apart. It is as if a sort of communal personality came into existence. Of course, it is not a real person: it is only rather like a person. But that is just one of the differences between God and us. What grows out of the joint life of the Father and the Son is a real Person, is in fact the Third of the three Persons who are God....this spirit of love, from all eternity, is a love going on between the Father and the Son.

I.D. The Gloriously Happy God. What this means is that God is a gloriously happy God. In fact, that is was the Apostle Paul writes in describing the Gospel in 1 Timothy 1:11—that it is the Good News of the gloriously happy God. The Greek word translated *happy* here is *makarios*, the same word translated *blessed* throughout the New Testament. And as we saw in the last chapter, the Greeks used it in reference to their gods. They called them "the blessed ones" because the Greeks believed that they had achieved a state of happiness and contentment that was beyond the cares, stress, worry, and problems of earth.

God, however, can only be infinitely happy or blessed by being entirely and completely, perfectly and eternally, self-sufficient in everything. Which means that God can only be infinitely happy or blessed in being love by being entirely and completely, perfectly and eternally, self-sufficient in His Triune love. God is infinitely happy or blessed precisely because He exists in a Triune Deity that overflows with pleasure, joy, delight, and happiness as the three Persons love, treasure, embrace, admire, and worship each other. God's pleasure, joy, delight, happiness, love, and worship is perfect and infinite. He neither created the universe nor planned Redemption out of need, but out of the overflow of His infinite happiness in His eternal triune love.

No other religion in the history of the world has a Triune God. Mormons don't. Jehovah Witnesses don't. Muslims don't. Hindus don't. Native Americans don't. The ancient Greeks and Romans, Babylonians and Egyptians didn't. Only the God of the Bible is a Triune God. Which means that only the God of the Bible can be both love and God. A solitary god cannot have the essential attribute of love. He may long to love, but it is impossible for him to be, in and of Himself, love. He may be taught by experience how to love, but he will always and forever love finitely and imperfectly. And therefore a solitary god cannot be God—because he will always have this deficiency. This imperfection. This flaw. This weakness. And a god with a deficiency, imperfection, flaw, and weakness cannot be God. A solitary god, therefore, is a logical impossibility;

even more of a myth than Big Foot, unicorns, and Santa Clause.

Imagine, however, if a god existed who was not infinitely happy in his love. He would be completely dependent on external factors for his happiness, which is the exact opposite of the Greek word for blessedness. He would be dependent on his creation to try to satisfy his longing to be happy. He would be worse then a needy, clingy boyfriend in his attempt to find love. And being imperfect, he would seek for love in all the wrong places. And failing to be fulfilled in love, he would become upset, angry, and wrathful. Such a god is not worthy of worship, love, or obedience, but only of fleeing as far away from as possible.

But because the God of the Bible is infinitely happy in His eternal Triune love, He is not dependent on anyone or anything for His happiness. He is entirely and completely, perfectly and eternally, self-sufficient in the Triune love of the Father, Son, and Holy Spirit and therefore has no needs. Consequently, He can love us without hypocrisy. Without flaw. Without pretense. Without dubious motives. His love is infinitely good and perfect, all the time; and all the time, His love is infinitely good and perfect. Therefore God can be trusted, loved, worshipped, and obeyed without reservation or hesitation.

II. Love is the Essence of Saving Faith. This, therefore, is why love is essential to saving faith. In order to be effective, in order to be genuine, in order to be operative, love must be the main thing of saving faith. For saving faith must first see, then saving faith must love what it sees.

II.A. Saving Faith Sees. First, saving faith must see Christ as irresistibly beautiful. In 2 Corinthians, chapter 4, we read:

> 3 But if also our gospel is veiled, it is veiled in those perishing— 4 in whom the god of this age did blind the minds of the unbelieving—that there does not shine forth to them the enlightening of the gospel of the glory of the Messiah, who is the image of God. 5 For we do not herald ourselves, but Messiah Jesus as Lord, and ourselves as your slaves because of Jesus. 6 Because it is God who said, "Out of darkness light is to shine," who did shine in our hearts for the enlightening of the knowledge of the glory of God in the face of Jesus Messiah.
>
> (2 Cor. 4:3-6 NYLT)

Here the Apostle describes conversion in two ways:
 • **Verse 4:** The light of the gospel of the glory of Christ, who is the image of God.
 • **Verse 6:** The light of the knowledge of the glory of God in the face of Jesus Christ.

Saving faith, therefore, is the illuminating work of the Holy Spirit. When the Holy Spirit regenerates or births from above someone, He first grants them eyes of faith to He who is invisible. Jesus Christ is currently reigning at the right hand of God the Father and, therefore, no one has seen Him face-to-face in nearly 2,000 years. Instead, the only way we see Christ is by having the eyes of our heart illumined so that we not only know things *about* Christ, but so that, more importantly, we *know* Christ. We no longer merely know biographical details of Jesus' life, but we know those details to be personally, intimately, and experimentally true. We see beyond a shadow of a doubt that Jesus is real and that He is irresistibly beautiful to us.

But look again at how this passage describes the object—the Person—we now see. Both verses 4 and 6 tell us that the light of the gospel—the illuminating work of the Holy Spirit as He gives us eyes of faith at the moment of conversion—reveal to us a glorious Christ. Saving faith, therefore, must see Christ as irresistibly glorious, or it is not saving faith. Saving faith must see Christ as supremely glorious, or it is not saving faith. Saving faith must see Christ as satisfactorily glorious, or it is not saving faith.

In short, saving faith sees all the beauties of God in the Person of Christ as incomparably glorious   It doesn't just see Jesus as a beautiful Savior without, for instance, also seeing Him as a beautiful Lord (Rom. 10:9; 1 Jn. 3:23). Saving faith does not divide Christ but sees Him equally glorious as Creator (Jn. 1:1-3), Sustainer (Col. 1:17; Heb. 1:3), Savior (Lk. 2:11), Teacher (Jn. 13:13), Guide (Acts 16:7), Comforter (Jn. 14:18, 27; 2 Cor. 1:5)), Helper (Phil. 1:19); Friend (Jn. 15:13-15); Advocate (1 Jn. 2:1); Protector (2 Thess. 3:3); Shepherd (Jn. 10) and Lord (Rom. 10:9). Anything less then this is not true, genuine saving faith but self-deceit.

II.B. Saving Faith Loves. Secondly, then, saving faith must love Christ as supremely glorious. Saving faith first grants us eyes of faith to see Christ as supremely glorious, then it naturally responds with love for Christ as supremely glorious.   If one's heart does not respond with love for Christ, then you are not seeing Him as supremely glorious. It is a logical impossibility.

And this is where our discussion of the eternal love of the Triune God is so vital to understanding saving faith as love. Earlier we saw that the Holy Spirit is the love birthed out of the mutual delight that has eternally existed between God the Father and God the Son. And it is the Holy Spirit —this Spirit of Love—that regenerates and indwells a believer, thereby enabling him to believe the Gospel. Turn with me, for instance, to John, chapter 3, beginning with verse 3:

> 3 Jesus answered and said to him, "Amen! Amen!—I say to you, if any one may not be born again from above, he is not able to behold the kingdom of God."
> 4 Nicodemus says to Him, "How is a man able to be born, being old? Is he able to enter a second time into the womb of his mother and to be born?"
> 5 Jesus answered, "Amen! Amen!—I say to you, if any one may not be born of water and the Spirit, he is not able to enter into the kingdom of God. 6 That which has been born of the flesh is flesh, and that which has been born of the Spirit is spirit.
>
> (Jn. 3:3-6 NYLT)

Jesus taught that a man can only be born again by the effectual working of the Holy Spirit. Or as the Apostle Paul put, we are saved "through the washing of regeneration

47

and renewing of the Holy Spirit" (Tit. 3:5). It is through the agency of the Holy Spirit whereby we are born again into Christ Jesus.

Therefore, since the Holy Spirit is the Spirit of Love between the Persons of the Triune God, and it is this Spirit of Love that regenerates a pagan into a believer, it must logically follow that at the moment of conversion God is loving God in us as we are converted through the work of the Holy Spirit.

Or, to put it another way, the Holy Spirit is the Person of the Trinity by which all three members of the Godhead love each other. And in regenerating someone, this Conduit of Divine Love inhabits our hearts. Out of natural, instinctive necessity, when this Spirit of Trinitarian Love opens our eyes to begin to see what He sees, we then also begin to love the Godhead as God loves the Godhead.

Or, to put it in yet a third and final way, the Holy Spirit loves through us; our hearts, in turn, become the conduit, albeit imperfectly, of divine love. God the Father loves God the Son through the Holy Spirit regenerating us. God the Son loves God the Father through the Holy Spirit regenerating us. Both God the Father and God the Son loves God the Holy Spirit through the Holy Spirit regenerating us. And God the Holy Spirit loves God the Father and God the Son through the Holy Spirit regenerating us. And in turn your heart begins to love the Triune God through the Holy Spirit regenerating you.

The essence of saving faith, therefore, refracts or reflects the love of the Triune God back to God. We see this confirmed in several places in Scripture. The first is in 1 John, which reads, "Whoever believes that Jesus is the Christ is born of God, and everyone who loves Him who begot also loves him who is begotten of Him" 1 Jn. 5:2).

Notice here that the Apostle John equates *believing* with *loving*, using them interchangeably: "Whoever believes...whoever loves."

The second reference comes from Jesus' High Priestly prayer the night before His crucifixion, where Jesus prays, "'And I have declared to them Your name, and will declare it, that the love with which You loved Me may be in them, and I in them'" (Jn. 17:26). Notice here that Christ describes regeneration as the act whereby the love with which God the Father has loved God the Son enraptures a believer's affections. Saving faith, therefore, occurs when a believer begins to love God the Son with a measure of the very same love that God the Father has for Him.

Furthermore, in the last chapter we saw that the essence of evil is to love sin more than to love God. The logical corollary, therefore, is that saving faith must love God more than sin. We see this confirmed by Christ in our third reference—in the 22nd chapter of Matthew:

> 34 And the Pharisees, having heard that He did silence the Sadducees, were gathered together unto Him. 35 And one of them, a lawyer, did question—tempting Him—saying, 36 "Teacher, which is the great command in the Law?"
>
> 37 And Jesus said to him, "'You shall agape the LORD your God with all your heart, and with all your soul, and with all your understanding.' 38 This is the first and great command. 39 And the second is like to it, 'You shall agape your neighbor as yourself.' 40 On these—the two

commands—all the Law and the Prophets
do hang."

(Matt. 22:34-40 NYLT)

Saving faith, therefore, must love God or it is sin. It must love God, or it cannot please God. It must love God, or it is disobedient. It must love God, or it is an idolater—for it must love God, or it is still in love with itself. Consequently, the essence of saving faith is love, or it is neither saving nor faith. This is why the Apostle Paul tells us that, "...now abide faith, hope, love, these three; but the greatest of these is love" (1 Cor. 13:13). Or why he tells us in Galatians 5:6 that faith works through love. Or, more literally, faith through love energizing. Love energizes faith. It gives life to faith. It gives it power. It makes it operative. Like electricity to a light bulb is love to faith. That is why love is the essence of saving faith. Without love, there is no faith. Love is the warp and woof of saving faith. Love is the main ingredient of faith.

This is why Jonathan Edwards, widely considered the greatest theologian America has ever produced, wrote in his sermon *Love, the Sum of All Virtue* (1738):

> That true love is an ingredient in true and living faith, and is what is most essential and distinguishing in it. Love is no ingredient in a merely speculative faith, but it is the life and soul of a practical faith. A truly practical or saving faith, is light and heat together, or rather light and love, while that which is only a speculative faith, is only light without heat; and, in that it wants spiritual heat or divine love, is in

vain, and good for nothing. A speculative faith consists only in the ascent of the understanding; but in a saving faith there is also the consent of the heart; and that faith which is only of the former kind, is no better than the faith of devils, for they have faith so far as it can exist without love, believing while they tremble. Now, the true spiritual consent of the heart cannot be distinguished from the love of the heart. He whose heart consents to Christ as a Saviour, has true love to him as such. For the heart sincerely to consent to the way of salvation by Christ, cannot be distinguished from loving that way of salvation, and resting in it. There is an act of choice or election in true saving faith, whereby the soul chooses Christ its Saviour and portion, and accepts of and embraces him as such; but, as was observed before, an election or choice whereby it so chooses God and Christ, is an act of love—the lore of a soul embracing him as its dearest friend and portion... So that it is love which is the active working spirit in all true faith. This is its very soul, without which it ; is dead as, in another form, he tells in the text, saying that faith, without charity or love is nothing, though it be to such a degree that it can remove mountains.

And Edwards is hardly alone in his assessment of saving faith as love-fueled, as the following quotes from other noted theologians attest:

- Calvin described saving faith as "a warm embrace of Christ" that consists in "pious affection."
- Turretin described faith as the "embrace of . . . that inestimable treasure."
- Owen called it a reception of the "Lord Jesus in his comeliness and eminency."
- Mastricht wrote that it "denotes desiring and reception with delight."
- Shedd wrote that "evangelical faith . . . involves an affectionate love of Christ."
- Berkhof described that it is a "hearty reliance on the promises of God."

Concluding Implications:

In conclusion, because God exists as a Trinity, saving faith must, of necessity, partake of the overflow of joy that the Triune God has in and of Himself. Saving faith joins in God's eternal triune love. Saving faith participates in God's infinite joy in being God. Saving faith reciprocates God's delight in being God. Saving faith receives and overflows with God's love as it is poured out into our hearts by the Holy Spirit (Rom. 5:5). Saving faith is being happy in God's infinite happiness in His eternal love.

The essence of saving faith is loving God supremely. And by the term *loving*, I am encompassing all of its naturally attendant synonyms as well: deep, heartfelt affection; endearment, devotion, adoration, worship, desire, ardor, yearning, besottedness, treasuring, enjoying, delighting in, appetite for, supreme satisfaction.

Therefore, this chapter is merely building upon the last by grounding affectionate saving faith in the Triune Godhead Himself. In God's happiness in being God. In the eternal, infinite, perfect love among the Trinity. Consequently, saving faith must be a coming to Christ, drinking of Christ, tasting of Christ, treasuring Christ, enjoying Christ, and loving Christ as one's supreme and fully satisfying joy. A coming to all of Christ as the complete satisfaction for the longings, desires, and carvings of one's soul. A loving all of God in Christ as beautiful—supremely, satisfactorily, gloriously, and irresistibly beautiful. A falling out of love with ourselves and the idols of our hearts and falling in love with God.

NATHAN W. TUCKER

3 THE END FOR WHICH GOD CREATED THE WORLD

I. *I*ntroduction—Why Do I Exist? In this chapter we are going to look at how affectionately loving saving faith—and only affectionately loving saving faith—glorifies God.   In order to do this, we must look at the reason why God created the world. Why did He create the universe? Why do we exist? What is the meaning and purpose of life?

A popular song a few years ago—a hit from the summer blockbuster *Barbie*—poignantly asks these questions:

> [1] I used to float, now I just fall down
> I used to know, but I'm not sure now
> What was I made for?
> What was I made for?
>
> [2] Takin' a drive, I was an ideal
> Looked so alive, turns out I'm not real
> Just somethin' you paid for
> What was I made for?
>
> [3] When did it end? All the enjoyment
> I'm sad again, don't tell my boyfriend
> It's not what he's made for
> What was I made for?
>
> Chorus: 'Cause I, I
> I don't know how to feel
> But I wanna try
> I don't know how to feel
> But someday, I might

Someday, I might

There are two questions that fallen, unregenerate men never ask themselves but shouldn't go to bed at night until they answer them. The first is how they—as totally depraved, rebellious creatures—can be reconciled, forgiven, and at peace with a holy and righteous God. Apart from the work of the Holy Spirit, no one ever asks themselves this question. They are so man-centered in their thinking that they audaciously assume that God will let bygones be bygones and let them—sin and all—into His heaven.

The second question that fallen, unregenerate mankind never asks is how they might glorify God. Apart from the regenerating work of the Holy Spirit, no one ever wakes up with the desire to magnify God's perfections. To give Him praise. To bring Him the most glory and honor, homage and worship. Only the power of God working in one's heart gives a person this desire to make much of God's infinite worth.

II. The Chief End of God. This passion to maximize the display of God's infinite worth is the very essence of who God is. For the chief end of God is to glorify Himself by enjoying Himself forever. Let me repeat that because it is so obnoxious to our sinful, prideful ears: the chief end of God is to glorify Himself by enjoying Himself forever. I will illustrate this with a simple five-question quiz before demonstrating it from Scripture.

1. Who is the most God-centered person in the universe?
Answer: God.

2. Who is uppermost in God's affections?
Answer: God.

3. Is God an idolater?

Answer: It is impossible for God to have any other god beside Himself for the simple reason that, by doing so, He would cease to be God.

4. What is God's passion?

Answer: To be loved, worshipped, feared, and obeyed as one's supreme treasure.

5. What, therefore, is the chief end of God?

Answer: The chief end of God is to glorify Himself by enjoying Himself forever.

Scripture teaches us over and over again that God only acts for the sake of His name, for the sake of His praise, for the sake of His glory, for His own sake (Is. 48:9-11; see also Ex. 14:4, 17-18, 36:22-23, 32; 1 Sam. 12:20, 22; 2 Kings 19:34, 20:6; Ps. 25:11, 106:7-8; Is. 43:6-7, 25, 49:3; Matt. 5:16; Jn. 7:18, 12:27-28, 13:31-32, 14:13, 16:14, 17:1; Rom. 3:25-26, 9:17, 15:7; Eph. 1:4-6, 12, 14; 1 Pet. 2:12). For Him to do otherwise would be to make Him less than God—an idolater who would profane His name by giving His glory to another (Is. 48:9-11; Ezek. 20:14). This universe does not exist for our sake. Eternity does not exist for our sake. We were not created to exist for our own sakes. Rather, everything was created to glorify God. To worship God. To magnify God. He is the supreme reality for which this life and the next exist.

II.A. God is Passionate for His Glory. Let's look at just a few examples of this principle at work in Scripture:

II.A.1. Creation. First, God is passionate for His glory in creation. Five times in Genesis 1 God calls His creation "good" (Gen. 1:4, 12, 18, 21, 25). And after God created Adam and Eve, He called it "very good" (vs. 31). When God stepped back and examined His work of creation, therefore, He was pleased and satisfied in His creative power. Psalm 104:31 tells us that Yahweh rejoices in His works. Why? Because David tells us in Psalm 19:1 that, "The heavens declare the glory of God; and the firmament shows HIs handiwork!" In other words, God delights in His creation because, and only because, it glorifies Him.

II.A.2. Call of Israel. Secondly, look at the reason why God created the Jewish people in the first place: in Isaiah, God tells Israel that, "'You are My servant, O Israel, in whom I will be glorified'" (Is. 49:3). Or as God explains in Jeremiah:

> "For as the belt cleaves to the loins of a man, so I caused to cleave to Me the whole house of Israel and the whole house of Judah," an affirmation of Yahweh, "to be to Me for a people, and for a name, and for praise, and for beauty, but they have not heard."
>
> (Jer. 13:11 NYLT)

God called Abraham out of Ur of the Chaldeans in order to make from his loins the Jewish people for God's own renown, praise, and glory.

II.A.3. Redemption of Israel. Third, this is the reason why God redeemed His people Israel from bondage in slavery through the Exodus. The psalmist, for instance, declares that:

> 7 Our fathers in Egypt have not considered wisely Your wonders;
> They have not remembered the abundance of Your steadfast love,
> But rebel by the sea, at the Red Sea.
> 8 Yet He saves them for His name's sake,
> To make known His might.
>
> (Ps. 106:7-8)

As you read the Bible, do not read passages like a string of unrelated pearls. Rather, the Bible—some parts more than others—builds a progressively logical argument from initial premise to ultimate conclusion. Therefore, always be on the look out for how the links in the chain of argument are connected by looking for words such as *therefore*, *because*, *for*, and *that*. In this passage, for instance, verse 7 tells us that the Israelites rebelled against God at the Red Sea when in unbelief they wished they were still back in slavery in Egypt (Ex. 14:11-12).

But then verse 8 tells us that nevertheless God still saved them. Why? "To make His might known." To maximize His glory in demonstrating His mighty power God parted the Red Sea so that He rebellious people might walk through on dry ground (Ex. 14:22). God's justice demanded that He Himself strike the Israelites dead for their rebellion or, at a minimum, that He let the Egyptians serve as the executioners. But God's righteousness—i.e., the relentless pursuit of His own glory—stayed His hand so that His glory would be maximized in providing a miraculous escape for His children. We see this confirmed in 2 Samuel where King David proclaims:

> "And who is as Your people, as Israel, the one nation in the earth whom God has gone to redeem to Himself for a people, and to make for Him a name, and to do for Yourself greatness—even fearful things for Your land, in the presence of Your people whom You has redeemed to Yourself out of Egypt, the nations and their gods?
>
> (2 Sam 7:23 NYLT)

We see this again in Exodus, where Yahweh tells Pharaoh, "'But indeed for this purpose I have raised you up, that I may show My power in you, and that My name may be declared in all the earth'" (Ex. 9:16). God decreed exactly who would be Pharaoh during the Exodus and hardened his heart precisely to demonstrate His unrivaled power so that His name would be glorified in all the earth. God didn't need ten plagues to bring His people out of Egypt. He could have started with the tenth plague and ended it with one blow. Or He could have started with the first plague but softened Pharaoh's heart so that he would let the Israelites go.

But God hardened Pharaoh's heart and sent plague after plague on Egypt in order to make a name for Himself. And one of the consequences of God's display of His glory is that Rahab the prostitute of Jericho was saved:

> [8] Now before they lie down, she has gone up to them on the roof [9] and says to the men, "I have known that Yahweh has

given you the land, and that your terror has fallen upon us, and that all the inhabitants of the land have melted at your presence. [10] For we have heard how Yahweh dried up the waters of the Red Sea at your presence, in your going out of Egypt, and that which you have done to the two kings of the Amorites who are beyond the Jordan—to Sihon and to Og— whom you devoted to destruction. [11] When we hear this, our hearts melt and there has not stood any more spirit in any man because of your presence, for Yahweh your God, He is God in the heavens above and on the earth beneath."

(Josh. 2:8-11 NYLT)

As a result of God's relentless pursuit of His glory in devastating Egypt with ten plagues and parting the Red Sea, this pagan harlot was converted and hid the two spies Joshua sent out to spy out the land of Canaan. And God rewarded her faith, for she became the great-grandmother of King David from whose line was born the God-man Jesus Christ as the long-promised Messiah of Israel.

II.A.4. Restoration of Israel. Fourth, God's passion for the maximization of His glory lead Him to exile, but not utterly destroy, Israel for their centuries-long disregard for His glory. For in Isaiah, God tells them:

[9] "For My name's sake I defer Mine anger,
And for My praise I restrain it for you
So as not to cut you off.

> [10] Behold!—I have refined you, but not as silver,
>
> I have chosen you for a furnace of affliction.
>
> [11] For My sake, for My own sake, I do it,
>
> For how should My name be polluted?
>
> And My glory to another I give not.
>
> (Is. 48:9-11 NYLT)

God's passion for His glory lead Him to mercy rather than the complete annihilation of the Jewish people.

II.A.5. Predestination. Five, God's unwavering pursuit of His chief end—to glorify Himself by enjoying Himself forever—led Him to predestine certain undeserving sinners to everlasting life. For God tells us that, "'Everyone who is called by My name whom I have created for My glory—I have formed him, yes, I have made him'" (Is. 43:7). Three times we are told in the first chapter of Ephesians that God "predestined us to adoption as sons by Jesus Christ to Himself" (vs. 5):

- **Verse 6:** "to the praise of the glory of His grace..."
- **Verse 12:** "...to the praise of His glory."
- **Verse 14:** "...to the praise of His glory."

Or as Peter tells believers: "But you are a chosen people, a royal priesthood, a holy nation, His own special people, that you may proclaim the praises of Him who called you out of darkness into His marvelous light" (1 Pet. 2:9). Our predestination to redemption, therefore, is solely "to the riches of His grace" (Eph. 1:7, 2:7). Or, to put it another way, our salvation is owing only to God's relentless pursuit of His glory.

II.A.6. Second Coming. Sixth and finally, God's passion for His glory is the reason for His second and triumphant coming, for the Apostle Paul tells us that Christ will come "in that Day to be glorified in His saints and to be admired among all those who believe" (2 Thess. 1:10). And at HIs coming the non-elect, unregenerate sinners will be deservingly cast into hell, for we are toldthat He predestined such vessels of wrath for destruction so "that He might make known the riches of His glory to the vessels of mercy which He had prepared beforehand for glory" (Rom. 9:23).

Conclusion. We have, therefore, seen that God is passionate for His glory in the creation of the Jewish people, redeeming them from Egypt, mercifully disciplining them, predestinating the elect unto salvation, and in His Second Coming and execution of judgment. And this is hardly an exhaustive survey of all the ways given in Scripture that God acts solely to maximize His own glory. For instance, in the book of Ezekiel alone God tells the Jewish people seventy-two times that He is acting, "so that you might known that I am Yahweh." Seventy-two times! And in ten other places in Ezekiel He simply declares, "I am Yahweh." Throughout the book of Ezekiel God promises both punishment and eventual restoration "that you may know that I am Yahweh." For instance:

- **33:29:** "'And they have known that I am Yahweh, in My making the land a desolation and an astonishment for all their abominations that they have done.'"

63

- **20:44:** "'And you have known that I am Yahweh, In My dealing with you for My name's sake, not according to your evil ways nor according to your corrupt doings, O house of Israel,' an affirmation of Adonai Yahweh."

To say, therefore, that God is passionate for His glory is an understatement. It would be far more accurate to say that God is jealous with a consuming fire for the fame of His name.

II.B. God is Jealous for His Glory. Over and over in Scripture God makes clear that He is jealous for His name, for His character, for His glory. (See generally Ps. 78:58, 79:5; Ezek. 38:19; Joel 2:18; Nahum 1:2; Zeph. 1:18, 3:8; Zech. 1:14, 8:2; 1 Cor. 10:22; James 4:5). In fact, Moses warns the Israelites that, "Yahweh your God is a consuming fire, a jealous God" (Deut. 4:24) for the reputation of His holy name (Ezek. 39:25).

Two chapters later Moses urges them to:

> [13] Yahweh your God you do fear, and Him you do serve, and by His name you do swear. [14] You do not go after other gods, of the gods of the peoples who are round about you, [15] for a zealous God is Yahweh your God in your midst, lest the anger of Yahweh your God burn against you and He has destroyed you from off the face of the ground.
>
> (Deut. 6:13-15 NYLT)

When Moses renews God's covenant with Israel at Moab, we read in Deuteronomy 29:

> [18] Lest there be among you a man or woman, or family or tribe, whose heart is turning today from Yahweh our God to go to serve the gods of those nations; lest there be in you a fruitful root of gall and wormwood. [19] Lest it has been, in hearing the words of this oath, that such a man blesses himself in his heart, saying, "I have peace, though I go on in the stubbornness of my heart." In order to end the fulness with the thirst. [20] Yahweh is not willing to be propitious to him, for then the anger and zeal of Yahweh smokes against that man. Lain down on him has all the oath which is written in this book, and Yahweh has blotted out his name from under the heavens. [21] Yahweh has separated him for evil, out of all the tribes of Israel, according to all the oaths of the covenant which is written in this Book of the Law."
>
> (Deut. 29:18-21 NYLT)

Three chapters later Moses predicts what will happen to Israel in the future:

> [15] And Jeshurun waxes fat and kicks: "You have been fat, you have been thick, you have been covered with fat." And he leaves God who made him and dishonors

the Rock of his salvation. [16] They make Him zealous with strangers, with abominations they make Him angry...

[18] You forget the Rock that begat you, and neglect the God who forms you. [19] And Yahweh sees and despises, for the provocation of His sons and His daughters. [20] And He says, "I hide My face from them, I see what is their latter end. For a froward generation they are, sons in whom is no steadfastness.

[21] They have made Me zealous by what is not god. They made Me angry by their vanities. And I make them zealous by those who are not a people. By a foolish nation I make them angry."

(Deut. 32:15-16, 18-21a NYLT; see also Ezek. 8:3-5).

Joshua, Moses' successor, warned the Israelites that:

[19] And Joshua says unto the people, "You are not able to serve Yahweh, for a God most holy He is; a zealous God He is. He does not bear with your transgression and with your sins. [20] When you forsake Yahweh, and have served gods of a stranger, then He has turned back and done evil to you and consumed you after He has done good to you."

(Josh. 24:19-20 NYLT)

Several centuries later we are told that, "Judah does evil in the eyes of Yahweh, and they make Him zealous above all that their fathers did by their sins that they have sinned" (1 Kings 14:22 NYLT). And in the book of Ezekiel, God compares Himself to a vengeful husband as He condemns the Israelites as an:

> Adulterous wife! You prefer strangers to Me—your own husband! All your detestable practices and your prostitution provoked me to anger with your increasing promiscuity. I turned away from you in disgust, yet you became more and more promiscuous. I will direct My jealous anger against you. I will sentence you to the punishment of women who commit adultery and who shed blood; I will bring upon you the blood vengeance of My wrath and jealous anger. I will put a stop to your prostitution, and you will no longer pay your lovers. 42 Then My wrath against you will subside and My jealous anger will turn away from you. Your lewdness and promiscuity have brought this upon you, because you lusted after the nations and defiled yourself with their idols.
> (paraphrase of Ezek. 16:22, 26, 32, 38, 41-42, 23:18-19a, 25, 29-30)

But though Israel stirred up God's jealous anger against them so that He drove them out of Palestine, His jealousy for His glory also brought them back from exile:

39 [25] Therefore, thus said Adonai Yahweh, "Now do I bring back the captivity of Jacob, and I have pitied all the house of Israel, and have been zealous for My holy name.".....

36 [5] Therefore, thus said the Adonai Yahweh, "Have I not, in the fire of My jealousy, spoken against the remnant of the nations and against all Edom who—with joy of the whole heart and spite of soul—gave My land to themselves for a possession for the sake of casting it out for a prey? [6] Therefore, prophesy concerning the ground of Israel, and you said to mountains and to hills, to streams and to valleys, thus said Adonai Yahweh, 'Behold!—I, in My jealousy, and in My fury, I have spoken because the shame of nations you have borne. [7] Therefore, thus said Adonai Yahweh, "I have lifted up My hand, 'Do not the nations who are with you from round about bear their own shame?'"'"

(Ezek. 39:25, 36:5-7 NYLT)

III. The Chief End of Man. The chief end of man, therefore, is to glorify God. This is the end for which God created the world—that we might glorify God for His mercies (Rom. 15:9).

III.A. God Doesn't Need Us. First, however, it cannot be stressed vigorously and often enough that God did not create the world because He *needed* to be glorified.

Rather, He created the world to magnify His glory. For instance, God declares in Psalm, chapter 50:

> [9] "I take not from your house a bull,
> Nor from your folds goats.
> [10] For Mine is every beast of the forest,
> The cattle on the hills of oxen.
> [11] I have known every bird of the mountains,
> And the wild beast of the field is with Me.
> [12] If I am hungry I will not tell you,
> For Mine is the world and its fulness.
> [13] Do I eat the flesh of bulls,
> And drink the blood of goats?
> [14] Sacrifice to God thanksgiving,
> And complete to the Most High you vows.
> [15] And call upon Me in the day of adversity;
> I deliver you, and you glorify Me.
>
> (Ps. 50:9-15 NYLT)

Or as God declared in Isaiah:

> [15] Behold!—nations as a drop from a bucket,
> And have been reckoned as small dust on the balance;
> Behold!—isles are as a small thing He takes up.
> [16] And Lebanon is not sufficient to burn,
> Nor its beasts sufficient for a burnt offering.

17 All the nations are as nothing before Him,

They have been reckoned by Him as nothing and emptiness.

(Is. 40:15-17 NYLT)

III.B. But God Demands Our Praise. But though God doesn't need anything from us, He does demand our praise. In teaching us how to pray, Jesus began with, "'Our Father, who are in heaven, hallowed be Your name'" (Matt. 6:9). In other words, the first and greatest request we are to make of every single prayer is for God to hallow—or make great, magnify, or glorify—His name (or fame or reputation) in all the earth.

In Philippians we are commanded to, "Rejoice in the Lord always, and again I say rejoice!" (Phil. 4:4). A chapter earlier, the Apostle Paul repeats his command to "rejoice in the Lord!" (Phil. 3:1). In 1 Thessalonians he again commands us to "rejoice at all times!" (1 Thess. 5:16). Throughout the Psalms we are repeatedly commanded:

- **Psalm 32:11**: "Be glad in Yahweh and rejoice, you righteous! And ing, all you upright of heart!" (NYLT).
- **Psalm 33:1**: "Sing, you righteous, in Yahweh..." (NYLT).
- **Psalm 37:4**: "And delight yourself on Yahweh..." (NYLT).
- **Psalm 104:1:** "Bless Yahweh, o my soul!..." (NYLT).
- **Psalm 105:1-5:**

1 Give thanks to Yahweh!
Call upon His name;
Make known among the peoples His acts!
2 Sing to Him, sing praise to Him;

Meditate on all His wonders!

³ Boast in His holy name;

The heart of those seeking Yahweh rejoice!

⁴ Seek Yahweh and His strength,

Seek His face continually.

⁵ Remember His wonders that He did,

His signs and the judgments of His mouth.

(NYLT)

• **Psalm 106:1:** "Praise Yah! Give thanks to Yahweh, for His steadfast love is good to the age!" (NYLT; see also Ps. 107:1).

We are commanded that, "...whether we eat or drink, or whatever we do, do all to the glory of God" (1 Cor. 10:31; see also Col. 3:17; 1 Pet. 4:11). Elsewhere we are commanded: "¹⁹ ...Sing[] and mak[e] melody in your heart to the Lord, ²⁰ giving thanks always for all things to God the Father in the name of our Lord Jesus Christ" (Eph. 5:19-20). In the Psalms God commands, "'Whoever offers praise glorifies Me'" (Ps. 50:23). And the list could go on and on. The command to rejoice in God, to praise God, to delight in God, to worship God, to sing to God is undeniably the most frequent command in Scripture. And since these are commands, not suggestions, the failure to obey them is sin. If we are not rejoicing in, praising, delighting in, worshipping, and singing to God, we are sinning.

III.C. Such a Duty of Delight is Loving. However, most people are turned off, slightly annoyed, and maybe even disgusted at a God who is jealous for our love, our worship, and our obedience. How, we might be tempted to

71

ask, is He not evil for being a narcissistic pig? In fact, God not only extolls His praises for all the world to see, but as we just saw He commands us to do likewise. How, therefore, is God not a vain, egotistical deity? One's gut-feeling response to God's demand for praise is probably the clearest litmus test as to whether they are, in fact, born again, regenerate believers. How we answer this question reveals the orientation of our heart—whether it is God-centered or still man-centered.

For instance, Erik Reece, a professor of environmental journalism, writing, and literature at the University of Lexington, wrote a book in which he called Jesus an egomaniac. When interviewed about that book, he elaborated: "Well, it just struck me as, who is this person speaking 2000 years ago, a complete historical stranger saying that we should love him more so than we should love our own fathers and sons? It just seemed incredibly egomaniacal."

C.S. Lewis, before his conversion, bulked at all the divine commands he found in the Psalms to praise God, writing that it sounded like God was "craving for our worship, like a vain woman who wants compliments." Oprah Winfrey, in reflecting upon her departure from the God of the Bible, reflected that:

> I was caught up in the rapture of that moment until he [the pastor] said jealous. And something struck me. I was 27 or 28, and I was thinking, "God is all. God is omnipresent. God is also jealous? A jealous God is jealous of me." Something about that didn't feel right in my spirit because I believe that God is love. And that God is in all things.

One last example comes from Brad Pitt, who was raised Southern Baptist, who in a 2007 interview for *Parade* magazine described how he, also, recoiled over God's commands to praise Him:

> I didn't understand this idea of a God who says, "You have to acknowledge me. You have to say that I'm the best, and then I'll give you eternal happiness. If you won't, then you don't get it!" It seemed to be about ego. I can't see God operating from ego, so it made no sense to me.

The problem is, God cannot be loving if He is not first and foremost for Himself. If He does not love, worship, treasure, and rejoice in His own infinite value and worth above all else, He is not God. By very definition, God must be the infinitely supremely valuable object imaginable. Therefore, should God stop loving, worshipping, treasuring, and rejoicing in Himself, He would be an idolater by instead bestowing His love, worship, treasuring, and rejoicing on another. He would commit blasphemy. He would deny His own infinite glory. And if God would worship something that is not god, then we, in turn, have no god worth worshipping. And if there is no god worth worshipping, then there is not god, and we might as well eat, drink, and be merry, for tomorrow we will die without hope.

But, by relentlessly pursuing His own glory above all other considerations, God is unfathomably good to us. We just saw earlier how His passion for His glory moved Him to create the universe, call out from among the nations the Jewish people, redeem them from bondage in Egypt, in mercy restoring them from exile, in predestining the elect unto salvation, and in His Second Coming. If God were not first and foremost for Himself, then none of these things would have occurred. If God did not relentlessly pursue His own glory above all else, there would have been no creation, no Cross, and no resurrection from the dead.

Or, to put it another way, God's passion for His glory means that God is passionate to display His infinite worth and value. Namely, to magnify His attributes of love, grace, mercy, patience, goodness, faithfulness, justice, wrath, etc. So when we say that God relentlessly pursues His own glory, we mean that He relentlessly pursues the display of His perfect and infinite love. Or He relentlessly pursues the display of His perfect and infinite grace. Or mercy. Or goodness. How, exactly, is that a bad thing? It would be the height of foolishness to tell God not to pursue His glory in displaying the infinite excellencies of His love. It is the epitome of insanity to tell God, "I think it is unloving that you are maximally loving."

Let's imagine, for instance, that you were a huge Celine Dion fan and spent quite a bit of money going to Vegas and buying a ticket to hear her perform. But once she was on stage, she simply read the lyrics to the audience. In disgust, someone asks her how this was possibly loving and honoring to her fans. She replied that she became convinced that it was unloving and selfish on her part to pursue her excellence in singing so now she merely reads the lyrics in a monotone voice. She had become convicted that it was prideful and arrogant to receive praise from her adoring fans, so she had stopped singing entirely.

Or imagine that you that you were about to board a plane, undergo brain surgery, or needed your car fixed.

How many of you would tell the pilot, surgeon, and car mechanic that you thought it was unloving for them to pursue a good reputation at their craft? Rather, would you not think that by pursuing their own excellence in their profession they were also loving to their customers? In fact, it was only by working hard to become experts in their fields that they were able to do their customers any good at all. If they had instead thought it was the height of arrogance to have a good reputation for excellence, they would be of no good to anyone at all, themselves included.

Similarly, therefore, it is only by treasuring Himself above everything else that God is able, in turn, to give us Himself as the greatest treasure imaginable for us to enjoy for all eternity.

III.D. Praise is Enjoyment's Appointed Consummation.

While C.S. Lewis had, before his conversion, stumbled over God's ego, he later realized the obvious, which he records in his book *Reflections on the Psalms*:

> The most obvious fact about praise —
> whether of God or anything — strangely
> escaped me. I thought of it in terms of
> compliment, approval, or the giving of
> honor. I had never noticed that all
> enjoyment spontaneously overflows into
> praise unless (sometimes even if) shyness
> or the fear of boring others is deliberately
> brought in to check it. . . .
> The world rings with praise — lovers
> praising their mistresses, readers their
> favourite poet, walkers praising the
> countryside, players praising their
> favourite game — praise of weather,

wines, dishes, actors, motors, horses, colleges, countries, historical personages, children, flowers, mountains, rare stamps, rare beetles, even sometimes politicians or scholars. . . .

I had not noticed either that just as men spontaneously praise whatever they value, so they spontaneously urge us to join them in praising it: "Isn't she lovely? Wasn't it glorious? Don't you think that magnificent?" The Psalmists in telling everyone to praise God are doing what all men do when they speak of what they care about. My whole, more general, difficulty about the praise of God depended on my absurdly denying to us, as regards the supremely Valuable, what we delight to do, what indeed we can't help doing, about everything else we value.

I think we delight to praise what we enjoy because the praise not merely expresses but *completes the enjoyment; it is its appointed consummation.* It is not out of compliment that lovers keep on telling one another how beautiful they are; *the delight is incomplete till it is expressed* (emphasis added).

Just think about this for a minute or two and his point becomes plainly obvious. For instance, can you remember the last time you attended a football game where the silence of the crowd enhance the joy and pleasure of being there? Or a time when a music concert was better without applause?   Or a movie comedy was more enjoyable without laughing?   Or a kiss was better without intimacy and love behind it?

In short, we praise God out of the overflow of our delight in Him as supremely and infinitely glorious.   The chief end of man, therefore, is to glorify God by enjoying Him forever. God created us solely to seek our joy in Him alone, and only to the extent that we do that do we glorify God.   Simply knowing things about God doesn't glorify Him; desiring God glorifies Him.   Simply seeing the beauties of God in the Person of Christ doesn't glorify God; treasuring Christ does.   Obeying every command in Scripture doesn't glorify God; loving Him with all our heart, soul, and mind does (Matt. 22:37).   Similarly, so to faith doesn't glorify God unless it is also accompanied by affection.

Concluding Implications:

In conclusion, this chapter is just simply building upon the previous chapters by grounding affectionate saving faith as necessary to glorifying God.   In order to glorify God, saving faith must be a coming to Christ, drinking of Christ, tasting of Christ, treasuring Christ, enjoying Christ, and loving Christ as one's supreme and fully satisfying joy. A coming to all of Christ as the complete satisfaction for the longings, desires, and carvings of one's soul. A loving all of God in Christ as beautiful—supremely, satisfactorily, gloriously, and irresistibly beautiful.   A falling out of love with ourselves and the idols of our hearts and falling in love with God.

4 ONLY AFFECTIONATE SAVING FAITH GLORIFIES

I.   In order to be saving, faith must boast in God's glory.   There is probably no better question to get to the bottom—the source—of your affections than this: do you feel more loved by God because (a) He makes much of you, or (b) because all that He does for you enables you to make much of Him?   Or, to put it another way, is the foundation of your joy the fact that God died for you so that you might escape hell, or is it that God died so that you might live forevermore to glorify Him?   Or, to put it yet another way, are you not only satisfied in, but passionate about, a God who loves you for His own Name's sake?

Let's break this down and make it more specific with the following self-assessment:

I.A.   Election.   The first question on this quiz is whether you rejoice that (a) God has made much of you by electing you before the foundation of the world, or (b) whether He has done so in order that you might make much of Him forever?   In Ephesians, chapter 1, we read:

> 3 Blessed is the God and Father of our Lord Jesus Messiah, who blessed us with every spiritual blessing in the heavenlies in Messiah, 4 just as He did choose us in Him before the foundation of the world, for our being holy and unblemished before Him in agape,5 having predestined us to the adoption of sons through Jesus Messiah to Himself, according to the good pleasure of His will,

(Eph. 1:3-5 NYLT)

Look at how much God makes of us in this passage:

- **Verse 3:** Blessed us with every spiritual blessing in the heavenly places.

- **Verse 4:** He choose us before the foundation of the world.

- **Verse 5:** Predestined us to adoption as sons.

Are these gifts the ultimate foundation of your joy? Test yourself by verse 6, which tells us the reason why God has freely and graciously made so much of us: "To the praise of the glory of His grace." Is that verse a problem for you? Does the fact that God has so lavishly poured out grace upon grace on you for the praise of *His* glory make you feel less loved? Does it make you feel jealous to know that everything God does for you He does not merely for your sake but, first and foremost, for His own sake? Do you feel bitter and envious that you are not the apple of God's eye after all, but that He is?

I.B. Justification. The second question of this self-assessment is whether you rejoice that (a) God has saved you, or (b) that God has done so for His own glory. The Apostle Paul tells us, "For the love of Christ compels us, because we judge thus: that if One died for all, then all died" (2 Cor. 5:14). Isn't that great news? For verse 14 tells us that in the death of Christ, all the elect have died to sin, guilt, and death! But then catch the reason provided by verse 15: "and He died for all, that those who live should live no longer for themselves, but for Him who died for them and rose again."

Does that divine motivation burst your bubble? Do you feel less loved by God because He didn't merely die to save you from sin, guilt, and the grave, but so that you might live forevermore for His glory and not for your own? Does it make you feel used by God? Or does it warm your heart to imagine heaven as a place where we will never have any less days to sing God's praise then when we first begun?

I.C. Sanctification.   The third question on this quiz is whether you feel more loved by God (a) because He cares for you and sanctifies you, or (b) because He does so for His own glory? In Philippians, chapter 1, we read:

> 9 And this I pray, that your agape may abound yet more and more in full knowledge and all judgment, 10 for your proving the things that are more valuable, that you may be pure and offenseless to the day of the Messiah, 11 being filled with the fruit of righteousness that is through Jesus Messiah, to the glory and praise of God.
>
> (Phil. 1:9-11 NYLT)

Look at all the wonderful gifts that Paul is praying that God will generously bestow upon the church at Philippi:
- **Verse 9:** Love may abound still more and more in knowledge and all discernment.
- **Verse 10:** That they may approve the things that are excellent.
- **Verse 10:** That they may be sincere and blameless.
- **Verse 11:** That they may be filled with the fruit of righteousness.

But then look at the end of verse 11 for the reason why God does all these things in the hearts of His children: "to the glory and praise of God." Does it annoy you that God is only working in your life as a believer for the glory and praise of His name? Does it bother you that He is making you into a better person for His praise, rather than your own? Do you feel less loved because your good works— your sanctification—are meant to reflect His righteousness rather than your own self-righteousness; His merit rather than your own; His goodness rather than your own? Or is it your heart's desire to throw whatever crowns He gives you back at His feet?

I.D. Christian Service. The fourth question of this self-assessment is whether you rejoice that (a) God has made much of you by putting you in the ministry, or whether (b) you rejoice that He has done so for His name's sake? For instance, in Romans 1 we read:

> [1] Paul, a slave of Jesus Messiah, a called apostle, having been separated to the gospel of God...[5] through whom we did receive grace and apostleship for obedience of faith among all the ethnic groups on behalf of His name.
>
> (Rom. 1:1, 5 NYLT)

God called and separated out Paul to be an apostle to all nations that they might be obedient to the faith. Why? The last part of verse 5 tells us that the reason God did so was "on behalf of His name." Does this bother you? Are you offended that God enlists you into His service, not so that you can make much of yourself, but so that you can make much of Him? Are you jealous that God calls and equips you to serve Him, not so you can make a name for yourself by being a famous preacher, or writing best-selling Christian books, or being a top-recording Christian artist, but so that you can make His name great? Why do you serve God—for your own glory in the praise of men or for His own glory in His praise by all men?

I.E. Heaven. The fifth and final question on this quiz is whether you feel loved by God more because (a) He allows you into heaven for all eternity, or (b) because He does so in order that you might enjoy Him forever? In 2 Thessalonians we find the Apostle Paul describing Christ's Second Coming as follows:

> [7] and to give you who are troubled rest with us in the revelation of the Lord Jesus from heaven with angelic messengers of His power,[8] in flaming fire, giving vengeance to those not knowing God, and to those not obeying the gospel of our Lord Jesus Messiah. [9] These shall suffer justice—destruction age-enduring—from the face of the Lord and from the glory of His strength, [10] when He may come in that Day to be glorified in His holy ones and to be wondered at in all those believing, because our testimony among you was believed.
>
> (2 Thess. 1:7-10 NYLT)

This is the consummation of the age—for when Christ returns His kingdom will be fully realized. He will cast death and Hades into hell. He will usher in the New Heavens and the New Earth. Peace will reign supreme.

There will be nor more death, or sorrow, or pain. There will be no more cancer. No more broken marriages and families. No more unemployment. No more war. Do you rejoice at that Paradise for it's own sake, or because it more fully enables you to, as verse 10 tells us, admire and glorify God?

I have found in my experience that a person's view of heaven is one of the single biggest indicators of whether they, in fact, have saving faith or merely intellectual head-knowledge. Whether they are simply using God as a genie in a bottle or whether they are truly born again into new creations that treasure Christ. Whether they are any different than Muslim terrorists who blow themselves up to get to heaven, not for the sake of enjoying their "god" Allah, but to get 70 virgins.

So ask yourself the following:

1. Do you merely rejoice at the hope of heaven as a place without any pain or misery, suffering or sorrow, as wonderful as that is?

2. Do you merely rejoice at the hope of heaven as a reunion with long-lost family members and friends from years gone by, as wonderful as that is?

3. Do you merely rejoice at the hope of heaven as having a mansion in glory, or walking streets of gold, or enjoying walks by the glassy sea, as wonderful as those things are?

All these things are true. And all these things are wonderful. But none of these things makes heaven heaven. No matter how enjoyable a pleasure is, by its ten-thousandth repetition it becomes almost painfully unbearable. Sex, for instance, is probably the greatest high humans can experience this side of heaven, and yet a hundred years of non-stop sex is, quite frankly, unappealing. All these things—no pain, being with family and friends, and streets of gold leading to mansions—as wonderful, pleasant, and enjoyable as they are, would by the end of a hundred years (or probably much sooner than that) become excruciatingly boring. Unbearably so. It would be like a vacation or family reunion that never ends and, sooner or later, leaves one weary of the monotony.

So how did you do on this self-assessment? Do you find yourself boating in God's glory, or hating it. Chaffing at it. Feeling less loved because you have to play second fiddle to God's relentlessly passionate pursuit of the fame of His name. Only faith that is supremely satisfied in a God who is passionate for His own glory saves.

II. In order to be saving, faith must magnify God's glory. This is the point that the Apostle Paul makes in 1 Corinthians 13—"the love chapter"—which reads:

> [1] If I speak with the tongues of men and of angelic messengers, but have not agape, I have become a sounding brass or a clanging cymbal. [2] And if I have prophecy, and know all the initiation mysteries and all knowledge, and if I have all faith, so as to remove mountains, but have not agape, I am nothing. [3] And if I give away all my goods to feed others, and if I give up my body that I may be burned, but have not agape, I am profited nothing...
> [13] And now there remains faith, hope, agape, these three; and the greatest of these is agape.
>
> (1 Cor. 13:1-3, 13 NYLT)

Look at what Paul is saying: though he may speak in tongues, or have the gift of prophecy, or have understanding and knowledge beyond all other men, or have enough faith to move mountains (Matt. 17:20), or give everything he owns to the poor, or die a martyr's death, but has not love, he is nothing. None of those things saves him. None of those things profit him in the least. Obedience without love is nothing. Spiritual gifts without love is nothing. Faith without love is nothing. Faith energized by love (Gal. 5:6), however, pleases God because it honors Him. Glorifies Him. Magnifies Him. Worships Him. Makes much of Him.

In Philippians, chapter 1, Paul describes what this type of loving, affectionate saving faith looks like:

> [19] For I have known that this shall fall out to me for salvation, through your heartfelt petition and the supply of the Spirit of Messiah Jesus, [20] according to my earnest expectation and hope that in nothing I shall be ashamed, but in all boldness, as always, so also now Messiah shall be magnified in my body, whether through life or through death. [21] for to me to live is Messiah, and to die gain. [22] But if I live on in the flesh, it is to me the fruit of work. But then what shall I choose I know not. [23] For I am pressed by the two, having the desire to depart and to be with Messiah, for it is far better. [24] But to remain in the flesh is more necessary on your account.
>
> (Phil. 1:19-24 NYLT)

For a number of years while living in Iowa I had PHIL121 as my license plate; it is easily one of my two favorite verses (the other being Galatians 2:20). Look with me first at verse 20, where Paul states that his earnest expectation and hope—his single-minded desire—is that Christ would be magnified in his body. The Greek word translated here as *magnify* (megaluno) means "to make or declare great." It is translated in other verses as *enlarge*, *exalt*, or *displaying greatness*. In other words, Paul wants Christ to be made much of—whether by his life or his death.

And then look at verse 21, where Paul tells us how Christ will be magnified in his life—"for to me, to live is Messiah, and to die gain." Let's focus on that last part first.

II.A. Death is Gain. How does Paul say that Christ will be magnified in his death? Because death is gain. But how in the world could the Apostle Paul tell us that death is gain? Death is the final goodbye. It is goodbye to a beloved spouse. Can you imagine telling your precious sweetheart of 50 years that you love them, but that death will be even better? It is goodbye to children, grandchildren, and great-grandchildren. It is goodbye to a great, fulfilling career. It is goodbye to a dream retirement. In short, death is goodbye to family and friends, dreams and hopes, ambitions and plans. How in the world, then, can death be gain?

What does Paul tell us? How does he tell us that death is gain? Look at verse 23, where he tells us that he has "the desire to depart [i.e., die] and be with Messiah." In other words, death is gain because it means the non-stop enjoyment of Christ Himself! What makes heaven heaven is God Himself! Teresa of Avila once said, "Wherever God is, there is heaven." As John Milton wrote,

"Thy presence makes our paradise, and where Thou art is heaven." Samuel Rutherford explained it this way, "O my Lord Jesus Christ, if I could be in heaven without Thee, it would be a hell; and if I could be in hell, and have Thee still, it would be a heaven to me, for Thou art all the heaven I want." As Randy Alcorn put it, "To be with God—to know Him, to see Him—is the central, irreducible draw of heaven."

J.I. Packer once wrote that: "The essence of eternity as I conceive it—as it lies before me as my destination—is quite simply the joy of being with the Lord." In his book *Knowing God*, he gave what is probably the best definition of heaven ever penned:

> What will make heaven to be heaven is the presence of Jesus, and of a reconciled divine Father who loves us for Jesus's sake no less than he loves Jesus himself. To see, and know, and love, and be loved by the Father and the Son, in company with the rest of God's vast family, is the whole essence of the Christian hope.

Christ is not a means to heaven; Christ is heaven. Therefore the Apostle Paul can say that death is gain because Christ was more precious to him than anything that life had to offer, or that death could take away. We see here, then, that saving faith must glorify God by treasuring Him more than health, wealth, and power. More than a good marriage, a good family, a good job. More than sex and entertainment, hopes and dreams, ambitions and plans. More than anything else imaginable.

II.B. To Live is Christ. Let us look at the first part of verse 21—how does Paul say that Christ will be magnified in his life? We will explore this answer more in depth in a future chapter, but for now we will look at the answer he provides in the third chapter of Philippians:

> 7 But what things were to me gains, these I have counted, because of Messiah, loss. 8 Yes, indeed, and I count all things to be loss, because of the excellency of the knowledge of Messiah Jesus my Lord, because of whom I suffered the loss of all things, and do count them to be dung, that I may gain Messiah, 9 and be found in Him, not having my own righteousness, which is of the law, but that which is through faith in Christ—the righteousness that is from God by faith; 10 to know Him, and the power of His resurrection, and the fellowship of His sufferings, being conformed to His death, 11 if anyhow I may attain to the resurrection of the dead.
>
> (Phil. 3:7-11 NYLT)

There is much in this passage, but let's focus on the answer provided by verse 8: "Yet indeed I count all things to be loss, because of the excellency of the knowledge of Messiah Jesus my Lord, because of whom I suffered the loss of all things, and do count them to be dung, that I may gain Messiah." That is how saving faith glorifies God—by counting all things that this world has to offer as loss, as rubbish, as refuse, as dung, as trash compared to knowing and enjoying Christ Jesus the Lord.

And we see this illustrated in the very next chapter in Philippians:

> 11 Not that I say it in respect of want, for I did learn in things in which I am to be content. 12 I have known both to be humbled and I have known to abound. In everything and in all things I have learned the initiation secret both to be full and to be hungry, both to abound and to be in want. 13 For in all things I have strength in Messiah's strengthening me.
>
> (Phil. 4:11-13 NYLT)

What is this secret of Christian contentment? That Christ is all we have. That He is more precious than all we could ever have. That He is more valuable than all we could ever lose. And therefore we can be content with nothing or with everything because Christ is our all in all. He is our life. This is why Paul can declare: "With Messiah I have been crucified, and live no more do I, but Messiah lives in me. And that which I now live in the flesh I live by faith in the Son of God, who agaped me and give Himself for me" (Gal. 2:20 NYLT). Not I, but Christ lives in me. This is how Christ is magnified in a believer's life.

II.C. Saving Faith, Without Affection, Does Not Glorify.
I want to be careful that I do not confuse the heartset of a mature believer with that of a new believer. Paul, for instance, speaks in Philippians 4:11 of having to learn this secret of Christian contentment. There is a sanctifying process in which God becomes more and more precious to a believer as the pleasures of this world grow increasingly

dim and dull to his sight. Nevertheless, the seeds of this secret that Paul learned were birthed in him at the moment he was regenerated from above by the Holy Spirit into a new creation. At conversion, the spiritual DNA of a new believer is indubitably stamped with an uncontrollable desire to magnify the worth and glory of God. Faith, therefore, that does not love God's glory cannot be saving faith.

Let me try to visualize this with a few examples. First, *faith* has often been used interchangeably with *trust* and illustrated with a chair example. Many an evangelistic sermon have told the audience that it isn't enough to look at and admire the chair, a symbol of Christ's atoning sacrifice. Rather, in order to be saved one has to sit on the chair. But how does that honor the chair if there is no love, no affection, no enjoyment in the transaction. Rather, the person sitting on the chair is simply using the chair to meet their needs for rest, for a place to sit down and relax. The chair, however, is not glorified because it is not treasured.

Or let's replace the chair with a father at the pool with his five-year-old son. He's standing in the pool encouraging his son to jump into his arms, assuring him that he will catch him. Now if the son responds, "Okay, Daddy, I'll jump in, but only because you are telling me to, not because I want to," the father receives no glory. But if the son instead replies, "Certainly, Daddy, because I trust you and want to show everyone else at the pool just how strong and trustworthy you are!", then the father is magnified.

One final illustration. Let's imagine that at my wedding, when the pastor asked me if I would take Lisa to be my lawfully wedded wife, I replied with a shrug of the shoulders and a, "I suppose." Or I struck from my vows the words, "to love and to cherish," because, after all, I was making a lifelong commitment to protect, care, and provide for. That should be enough, all this mushy emotionalism was just a little overboard for my tastes. Such an attitude hardly honors my wife. Magnifies her. Glorifies her. It merely treats her like a business transaction in which I'm the breadwinner and she's the housekeeper. But if instead I had said, "I treasure her so much that I will spend my life dying to myself so that I might love and cherish her as I do myself," then she is rightly made much of.

In the same way, faith that does not carry the seeds of desire to make much of God, whether by life or by death, because He is the believer's treasure cannot be saving faith.

III. In order to be saving, repentance must treasure God's glory.
Finally, repentance cannot be saving repentance unless it treasures God's glory.

III.A. Saving Repentance is Turning To God From Sin.
Repentance and faith are two sides of the same coin called conversion. You cannot have one without the other; they are inseparable. If you have faith without repentance, you do not have saving faith. You merely have head knowledge without godly sorrow for your sinfulness. And if you have repentance without faith, you do not have saving faith. Rather, you have remorse without hope; penitence without assurance. In fact, these two terms—repentance and faith—are used interchangeably in the New Testament for saving faith.

These two terms—repentance and faith—are synonymous for new birth:

- **Mark 1:15:** "Repent and believe the Gospel!"

- **Acts 20:21:** "Repentance towards God and faith toward our Lord Jesus Christ."
- **Acts 26:19:** "Repent, turn to God, and do works befitting [or worthy] of repentance."
- **1 Thess. 1:9:** "Turn to God from idols."

Saving faith, therefore, is a turning to Christ in belief as one forsakes and repents of their sins. You cannot have one without the other, or you do not have saving faith. Genuine faith, authentic faith, saving faith is a penitent faith.

What, then is repentance? There is an impostor faith in which a professing Christian embraces Christ as their ticket out of hell, but nothing more. They come under just enough conviction of sin to know they are not at peace with God and, consequently, in danger of hell fire upon drawing their last breath. But the problem with their repentance is that they don't actually hate their sins, they just simply don't want to go to hell. And if it were possible, they would still want their sins if they could still escape hell. Sadly, their conviction of sin is merely that of worldly sorrow—that of a criminal sorry that he got caught but who would do it again in a heartbeat if he thought he could get away with it.

III.B.   Godly sorrow, in contrast, is rooted and grounded in love for God. It is when the Holy Spirit opens the eyes of the heart through new birth and an individual sees God as holy and righteous, just and good, loving and wrathful. He sees God as worthy of all of his love, worship, and obedience. He sees God as the most supremely valuable treasure in the entire universe, and cries out like the angels before the throne of God in Isaiah 6, "Holy, Holy, Holy is Yahweh Sabaoth!" (Is. 6:3 NYLT).

And at the same time he sees himself as a wretched and vile sinner without any defense or justification before such a holy God. Like Isaiah the prophet who in a vision saw God seated in Hs throne room in Isaiah 6, a penitent man cries out, "Woe is me, for I am a man with an unclean heart!" (Is. 6:5). And like the crowds at Pentecost who were stabbed through the heart with godly sorrow, he cries out, "What must I do to be saved?!" (Acts 2:37). And like the Old Testament saints in Joel, he rends his heart and turns to God with all of his heart (Joel 2:12-13).

At the moment of new birth, the Holy Spirit begets or creates in him a new nature. As 2 Corinthians 5:17 proclaims, "..."if anyone is in Messiah, he is a new creation: old things have passed away, behold!—all things have become new!" (NYLT). He now loves the God he once hated, and hates the sin he once loved. He has experienced nothing less than a heart transplant.

III.B.1. But the lynch pin for saving repentance is first beholding God as the most supremely valuable Being in the universe. It is seeing God as glorious. As worthy. As desirable. As enjoyable. Supremely so. Saving repentance is birthed out of first treasuring God. It arises from seeing God's excellencies—His holiness, His justice, His love, His mercy, His grace. And such a sight can only bring pleasure and joy, which then produces grief and sorrow over having wronged and blasphemed such a worthy Being. Repentance is nothing less than sweat sorrow; and the more pleasure one has in God, the more sorrow of sin it produces.

To illustrate, let's say that I got angry at my wife and said harsh words to her that brought her to tears. What leads me to repent of my temper? Is it because my conscience condemns me? Yes, certainly, in part. Yes it because God's Word condemns me? Yes, certainly, in part. Is it because I want to be a good example to our children? Yes, certainly, in part. And there could be a handful of other considerations that play a role. But the primary motivating factor that would lead me to repentance (other than my love for God) is my love for my wife. It is seeing how beautiful, precious, and worthy she is to be treasured, and how vile and wretched I am at not doing so. In the same way, repentance towards God is—at it's deepest, most fundamental, and persevering level— motivated by love for God. Anything less is simply motivated by a criminal sorry he got caught, but not sorry at his crime.

III.B.2. Or, to put it another way, you cannot have remorse for something—or, in this case, Someone—you don't want. You must first want and desire God in order to repent for exchanging His glory for that of the idols of your heart. If, however, you do not love Christ, desire Christ, treasure Christ, then you are still an idolater. You cannot be repentant if you still treasure something other than God.

CONCLUDING IMPLICATIONS:

In conclusion, in order to be saving, faith must glorify God by loving Him. This chapter is just simply building upon the previous chapters by grounding affectionate saving faith as necessary to glorifying God. In order to be saving, faith must glorify God by coming to Christ, drinking of Christ, tasting of Christ, treasuring Christ, enjoying Christ, and loving Christ as one's supreme and fully satisfying joy. A coming to all of Christ as the complete satisfaction for the longings, desires, and carvings of one's soul. A loving all of God in Christ as beautiful—supremely, satisfactorily, gloriously, and irresistibly beautiful. A falling out of love with ourselves and the idols of our hearts and falling in love with God.

5 JOY IN YAHWEH IS OUR STRONGHOLD

*I*n the previous chapters we have seen from Scripture how love for God must be an essential component of saving faith for the following four reasons:

1.   Because the totality of Scripture defines it that way —as a coming and tasting, a receiving and loving, a seeing and treasuring, a drinking and enjoying the Person of Christ.

2.   Because God exists as a Trinity, saving faith must, of necessity, partake of the overflow of joyous love that the Triune God has in and of Himself.

3.   Because only faith that loves God can possibly glorify God.

4.   Because godly sorrow over sin leading to genuine saving penitent faith can only be grounded in love for God.

Now, in this chapter and the next, we will see the fifth and final reason—that only love-fueled faith perseveres through the trials and sufferings of this life.   For this understanding of salvation is vital to our everyday Christian lives. The maximization of our joy in Christ is critical to our walk of sanctification and obedience. Delighting in God is an essential ingredient in our perseverance of faith until our final breath.

For despite all this talk of joy, desire, delight, and love, this doctrine is not a naive doctrine. It is not a doctrine of blithe happiness in the face of sin, sorrow, and death. It is not a doctrine of indifferent delight that turns a deaf hear to all the heartache and suffering in the world.   It is not a chipper joy. No, saving faith is a doctrine of serious joy. Of joy in suffering. Of sorrowful yet always rejoicing (2 Cor. 6:10).

What is going to sustain your faith when you lose your job? When the next Great Depression comes? When the next World War begins?   When you have to bury your spouse of fifty years? When you get the phone call from the doctor with the test results that you have terminal, excruciatingly painful bone cancer with only months to live? When your woken up at 2:00 in the morning by the police who report that your only daughter and her unborn child were killed in a car accident?   Will your faith be shaken and falter, never to be recovered?

I.   Do you have any depth and root?   In Matthew, chapter 13, we read:

> 3 And He spake to them many things in parables, saying: "Behold!—the sower went forth to sow. 4 And in his sowing, some indeed fell by the way, and the birds did come and devour them. 5 And others fell upon the rocky places where they had not much earth, and immediately they sprang forth because of not having depth of earth. 6 And the sun having risen they were scorched, and because of not having root they withered. 7 And others fell upon the thorns, and the thorns did come up and choke them. 8 And others fell upon the good ground and were giving fruit, some indeed a hundredfold, and some sixty, and some thirty. 9 He who is having ears to hear -- let him hear!"...

[18] "You, therefore, hear the parable of the sower: [19] Everyone hearing the word of the kingdom and is not understanding, then the evil one comes, and catches that which has been sown in his heart. This is that sown by the way. [20] And that sown on the rocky places, this is he who is hearing the word and immediately with joy is receiving it, [21] yet he has no root in himself, but is temporary. For persecution or tribulation having happened because of the word, immediately he is stumbled. [22] And that sown toward the thorns, this is he who is hearing the word, and the anxiety of this age and the deceitfulness of the riches do choke the word, and it becomes unfruitful. [23] But that sown on the good ground, this is he who is hearing the word and is understanding, who indeed bears fruit and makes, some indeed a hundredfold, and some sixty, and some thirty."

(Matt. 13:3-9, 18-23 NYLT)

In this parable Jesus is describing the Gospel reception by various types of professing believers. Here we are concerned about those who fell on stony places in verses 5-6 and 20-21. These are not Redwoods. Not by a long shot. Rather, Christ describes them as having "no depth" (vs. 5) and "no root" (vs. 21). They heard the Gospel (vs. 20), they received it with apparent joy (vs. 20), but when they face "tribulation or persecution" because they claim to be Christians (vs. 21), they immediately stumble (vs. 21) and wither away (vs. 6) because they had no root (vs. 6, 21).

Do you have any root? What is going to sustain your faith when trials and tribulations come your way? Scripture is NOT the Prosperity Gospel. It does not preach that Christ is a pimp daddy who promises health, wealth, and power; who guarantees you your best life now. Rather, it is just the opposite. For in John 16:33, Jesus assures His elect that in this world they will have many tribulations (see also Matt. 10:24-25, 24:9; Jn. 15:18-21, 16:3), and in Acts 14:22 Paul tells us that it is only through such trials that we must enter the kingdom of God (see also 1 Pet. 4:12).

Do you, therefore, have a faith that will persevere to the finish line, come what may? Remember that the psalmist proclaims that, "In Your presence is fulness of joy, and at Your righthand are pleasures forevermore!" (Ps. 16:11). Not partial joy. Not temporary pleasures. But 100% joy now and forever! So how can we reconcile this precious reality of fulness of joy forever in God with the suffering and sorrow that we all face?

The secret of the Christian life—what sets it apart from any other religion or ethic—is what the Apostle Paul writes in 2 Corinthians 6:10—we are "sorrowful, yet always rejoicing." Seem impossible?

II. Sorrowful, Yet Always Rejoicing. Let us look at several examples from Scripture of this seemingly paradoxical faith—faith that rejoices in suffering.

II.A. The first is found in Job, chapter 1, which reads:

> 13 And the day is that his sons and his daughters are eating and drinking wine in the house of their brother, the first-born.

¹⁴ And a messenger has come in unto Job and says, "The oxen have been plowing, and the donkeys feeding by their sides, ¹⁵ and Sheba falls upon them to take them, and the young men they have smitten by the mouth of the sword, and I am escaped—only I alone—to declare it to you."

¹⁶ While this one is speaking, another also has come and says, "Fire of God has fallen from the heavens, and burns among the flock, and among the young men, and consumes them, and I am escaped—only I alone—to declare it to you."

¹⁷ While this one is speaking, another also has come and says, "Chaldeans made three heads of companies to rush on the camels and take them, and the young men they have smitten by the mouth of the sword, and I am escaped—only I alone — to declare it to you."

¹⁸ While this one is speaking another also has come and says, "Your sons and your daughters are eating and drinking wine in the house of their brother, the first-born. ¹⁹ And behold!—a great wind has come from over the wilderness and strikes against the four corners of the house, and it falls on the young, and they are dead. And I am escaped—only I alone—to declare it to you."

²⁰ And Job rises, tears his robe, shaves his head, and falls to the earth, and

prostrates himself in worship. 21 And he says,

"Naked came I forth from the womb of my mother,
And naked I turn back thither.
Yahweh has given and Yahweh has taken:
Let the name of Yahweh be blessed."

22 In all this Job has not sinned, nor attributed folly to God.

(Job 1:13-22 NYLT)

Job lost everything except his wife and, up to this point, his health. And yet what did Job do? Verse 20 tells us that he "prostrates himself in worship." Verse 21 tells us that he blessed the name of Yahweh. And verse 22 tells us that he did not charge God with any wrongdoing for brining these disasters upon him. How? And do you have a faith that would enable you to do likewise?

II.B. The second example comes from 2 Kings, chapter 4, where we find the story of Elisha the prophet praying that a barren woman would bear a son. She did so, but then we pick up the story in verse 18:

18 And the lad grows, and the day comes that he goes out unto his father, unto the reapers. 19 And he says to his father, "My head, my head" And he says to the young man, "Bear him unto his mother."
20 And he bears him and brings him in unto his mother, and he sits on her knees till the noon and dies. 21 And she goes up and lays him on the bed of the man of God, and shuts the door upon him, and

goes out [22] and calls to her husband and says, "Send, I pray you, to me one of the young men and one of the donkeys, and I run unto the man of God and return."

[23] And he says, "Why are you going unto him today? It is neither the new moon nor sabbath?" And she says, "Shalom!" [24] And she saddles the donkey and says unto her young man, "Lead, and go, do not restrain your riding for me, except I have said so to you."

[25] And she goes and comes in unto the man of God, unto Mount Carmel, and it comes to pass, at the man of God seeing her afar off, that he says to Gehazi his young man, "Behold!—this Shunammite! [26] Now, run, I pray you, to meet her and say to her, "Is there shalom with you? Is there shalom with your husband? Is there shalom with the child?" And she says, "Shalom!"

[27] And she comes in unto the man of God on the hill, and lays hold of his feet, and Gehazi comes near to thrust her away. But the man of God says, "Let her alone, for her soul is bitter to her, and Yahweh has hidden it from me, and has not declared it to me."

(2 Kings 4:18-27 NYLT)

So you have the Shunammite woman's faith to be simultaneously "bitter" (vs. 27) while also experiencing "shalom" (vs. 26)? The Hebrew word *shalom* means, literally, *peace*, though the NIV84 translates it as "'everything is all right'" and the NKJV as "'it is well.'"

Henrietta, the wife of R.C. Ryle (who was the Bishop of Liverpool 130 years ago), had verse 26—"It is well"— written on her tombstone. Do you have the faith to have such a testimony? This is also the verse on which Horatio Stafford based his hymn *It Is Well With My Soul*! Do you have the faith to see four daughters drown at sea like he did while simultaneously confessing that it is well with your soul?

II.C. The third example is found in Luke, chapter 6, where we find the Beatitudes of Jesus' Sermon on the Plain:

> [22] "Blessed are you when men shall hate you,
> And when they shall separate you for exclusion,
> And shall reproach you,
> And shall cast forth your name as evil,
> For the Son of Man's sake.
> [23] Rejoice in that day and leap!
> For behold!—your wage is great in the heaven,
> For according to these things their fathers were doing to the prophets.
>
> (Lk. 6:22-23 NYLT)

Unlike the seed that fell on stony ground, when trials and tribulations come our way we are to rejoice and leap for joy! And not in a future day, but in the very day that those trials and tribulations come—"rejoice *in that day*"! Jacob, the half-brother of Jesus, tells us to, "count it all joy when you fall into various trials!" (Jac. 1:2) Peter tells us to rejoice the fiery trials which come our way (1 Pet. 4:12-13). How is this possible?

But we see that the early church did, in fact, know how to do this. For instance, when the Twelve Apostles were imprisoned and beaten by the Jewish religious authorities for preaching in the name of Jesus, "they departed from the presence of the council, rejoicing that they were counted worthy to suffer shame for [Jesus] name" (Acts 6:41). Acts 16 tells us that Paul and Silas were severely beaten with rods (vs. 22-23) and then thrown into the deepest, darkest cell with their feet fastened in the stocks (vs. 24). And yet, verse 25 tells us that even as late as midnight Paul and Silas were praying and singing hymns to God! Do you have such a faith, at least in seed form, that will rejoice and leap for joy when disaster strikes and all hope seems hopeless?

II.D. The fourth example comes from 2 Corinthians, chapter 8, where the Apostle Paul is describing to the Corinthian church the generosity of the church at Philippi to the poor and needy of the Jerusalem church. Beginning with verse 1 we read:

> [1] And we make known to you, brethren, the grace of God that has been given in the assemblies of Macedonia, [2] because in much trial of tribulation the abundance of their joy and their deep poverty did abound to the riches of their generosity. [3] Because I testify that, according to their power, and above their power, they were willing of themselves, [4] begging us with much entreaty to receive the grace and

the fellowship of the deaconing to the
saints.

(2 Cor. 8:1-4 NYLT)

Despite "much trial of tribulation" and "deep
poverty" (vs. 2), Paul tells us that their joy abounded all the
more, resulting in the "riches of their generosity" (vs. 2) in
which they freely gave above their means (vs. 3). Do you
have this type of faith to abound in joy in the face of "much
trial of tribulation" and "deep poverty"?

II.E. The fifth and final example comes from the Apostle
Paul himself. Turn with me to 1 Corinthians 4 where Paul
gives a brief autobiographical sketch of his trials and
tribulations as a missionary church planter:

> 9 For I think that God did set forth us, the
> apostles, last—as appointed to death,
> because we became a theater exhibition
> to the world, both angelic messengers and
> men. 10 We are fools because of Christ,
> but you wise in Christ! We are without
> strength, but you are strong! You are
> glorious, but we are dishonored! 11 Unto
> the present hour we both hunger and
> thirst, and are naked, and are struck with
> fists, and wander about homeless. 12 And
> we labor, working with our own hands.
> Being reviled, we bless; being persecuted,
> we forbear; 13 being spoken evil of, we
> entreat; as filth of the world we did
> become as filth of the world, the scum of
> all things until now.

(1 Cor. 4:9-13 NYLT)

2 Corinthians, chapter 11, provides us in even fuller glimpse into his sufferings and persecutions:

> 23 Are they deacons of Messiah?—as beside myself I speak—I more; in labors more abundantly, in stripes above measure, in prisons more frequently, in deaths many times. 24 From Jews five times I received forty stripes minus one. 25 Three times was I beaten with rods; once was I stoned; three times I was shipwrecked; a night and a day I have passed in the deep; 26 in journeys many times, in perils of rivers, in perils of robbers, in perils from kindred, in perils from ethnic groups, in perils in the city, in perils in the wilderness, in perils in the sea, in perils among false brethren; 27 in labor and painful toil, in sleeplessness many times, in hunger and thirst, in fastings many times, in cold and nakedness; 28 apart from the things external, the pressure upon me daily is the care of all the assemblies. 29 Who is infirm, and I am not infirm? Who is stumbled, and I am not on fire?
>
> (2 Cor. 11:23-29 NYLT)

Finally, in Romans, the Apostle Paul tells us that he has "great sorrow and continual grief in my heart" for his Jewish brethren who are not saved (Rom. 9:2). This isn't just "great sorrow and...grief" only during times of imprisonment, beatings, and hardships. No, Paul specifically states that this is "continual" sorrow and grief. And yet, in Philippians this same Paul tells us, "Rejoice in the Lord always! Again, I will say, rejoice!" (Phil. 4:4). Do you have that kind of persevering faith that rejoices always, even in the midst of heart-wrenching sorrow?

III. Joy in Yahweh is Our Stronghold. Joy in sorrow is not a contradiction. It is not the death knell of saving faith. Rather, it is the only thing that will sustain your faith when all your world falls away around you. I'm not talking about hope in future joy, though we have promise after promise guaranteeing that in Scripture. In Revelation, for instance, we are promised that "God will wipe away every tear from their eyes; there shall be no more death, nor sorrow, nor crying. There shall be no more pain, for the former things have passed away" (Rev. 21:4). Or in 2 Corinthians, chapter 4, the Apostle Paul tells us:

> [16] Therefore, we faint not, but though our outward man decays, yet the inward is renewed day by day. [17] For the momentary lightness of our tribulation works for us a surpassing upon surpassing weight of glory age-enduring. [18] We are not looking to the things seen, but to the things not seen; for the things seen are temporary, but the things not seen are age-enduring.
>
> (2 Cor. 4:16-18 NYLT)

Those promises are beautiful and precious—no more pain, no more death, no more crying, a far more exceeding and eternal weight of glory! But they are not what this sermon is about. Rather, we are looking at how exactly a genuine, born-again believer can simultaneously have joy even in the midst of heart-wrenching loss and sorrow. Not comfort in promisees of future joy. But present-tense joy in the here and now in suffering, pain, and grief. Remember that Psalm 16:11 promises us that, "In Your presence is fulness of joy, and at Your righthand are pleasures forevermore!" We are looking at how that can be. How all these individuals we just looked at could both rejoice and grieve at the same time.

The title of this chapter comes from Nehemiah 8:10, in which Nehemiah told the weeping people, "...be not grieved, for the joy of Yahweh is your stronghold!" (NYLT). While much can, and probably should, be said on this topic, we will look at but three ways in which the joy in Yahweh is our stronghold in suffering.

III.A. First, the joy in Yahweh is our stronghold in suffering because our sufferings are Christ sufferings. This sounds almost blasphemous. Almost too good to be true. But Paul tells believers that they "suffer with Him [Christ], that we may also be glorified together *with Him*" (Rom. 8:17). In another place he tells us that "the sufferings of Christ abound in us" (2 Cor. 1:5). Still elsewhere he tells us that he considers his life of self-righteousness and self-merit to be rubbish so "that I might know Him [Christ]...and the fellowship of His sufferings" (Phil. 3:10). Finally, Peter tells us to "[13] rejoice to the extent that you participate of Christ's sufferings...[14]...blessed are you, for the Spirit of glory and of God rests upon you" (1 Pet. 4:13-14).

Our sufferings are, in fact, Christ's sufferings:
- We suffer with Christ (Rom. 8:17).
- Christ's sufferings about in us (2 Cor. 1:5).
- We have fellowship in His sufferings (Phi. 3:10).
- We participate in Christ's sufferings (1 Pet. 4:13).

109

Now Scripture provides two grounds for these audacious statements. The first is that when we are persecuted for being believers, our persecutors are really persecuting Christ. We see this most clearly when the risen Christ appeared to the Apostle Paul on the Damascus road. Up until this moment Paul was not a believer but was instead a fire-breathing persecutor of believers on his way to Damascus to kill and imprison Christians. But Jesus appeared to him and said, "'Saul, Saul, why are you persecuting Me?'" (Acts 26:14). Not, "Why are you persecuting the Church?" Not, "Why are you persecuting Christians?" But, "Why are you persecuting Me?" So Christ Himself is suffering persecution along with us when we are persecuted for the sake of His name.

But the second reason why our sufferings are, in fact, Christ's sufferings is our union with Christ. Galatians 2:20 tells us that though we live, yet it is not us who live but Christ in us. Similarly, Colossians 3:3-4 tells us that our life is hidden with Christ in God and, therefore, He is now our life. Ephesians 5:30-32 tells us that, as Christ's Bride, we are members of His body—flesh of His flesh and bone of His bones—for the two shall become one flesh.

Therefore, whether our sufferings are the result of religious persecution or the result of living in a fallen world —Christ suffers with us. Our sufferings are His sufferings. He is not participating in our sufferings, but rather we are participating in His. When we wept, He has already wept first. When we experience pain, He already experienced it first. When our hearts are breaking, His heart already broke with grief. For Isaiah 53:4 tells us that Christ bore our grief and carried our sorrows.

But through the storm of our grief and pain upon Calvary, Christ emerged victorious and is therefore able to comfort us. 2 Corinthians, chapter 1, reads:

> [3] Blessed is God—the Father of our Lord Jesus Messiah and the Father of mercies and God of all comfort—[4] who is comforting us in all our tribulation, for our being able to comfort those in any tribulation through the comfort with which we are comforted ourselves by God. [5] Because, as the sufferings of the Messiah abound to us, so through the Messiah also abounds our comfort.
>
> (2 Cor. 1:3-5 NYLT)

Therefore, just as our sufferings are Christ's sufferings, so His comfort is now also our comfort! He draws close to us, surrounds us with His loving arms, and gives us the peace of His presence. John Patton was a missionary in the 1800s to the cannibals of the New Hebrides. After years of largely futile ministry on one of the islands, the majority of the Natives sought his life. A few of them, however, told him to climb a tree while they distracted and mislead those who hunted his life. The following is his account of that night in his autobiography:

> Being entirely at the mercy of such doubtful and vacillating friends, I, though perplexed, felt it best to obey. I climbed into the tree and was left there alone in the bush. The hours I spent there live all before me as if it were but of yesterday. I heard the frequent discharging of

muskets, and the yells of the Savages. Yet I sat there among the branches, as safe as in the arms of Jesus. Never, in all my sorrows, did my Lord draw nearer to me, and speak more soothingly in my soul, than when the moonlight flickered among those chestnut leaves, and the night air played on my throbbing brow, as I told all my heart to Jesus. Alone, yet not alone! If it be to glorify my God, I will not grudge to spend many nights alone in such a tree, to feel again my Savior's spiritual presence, to enjoy His consoling fellowship. If thus thrown back upon your own soul, alone, all alone, in the midnight, in the bush, in the very embrace of death itself, have you a Friend that will not fail you then?

Intimate fellowship in the comforting presence of our Savior and Friend is the first reason why joy in Yahweh is our stronghold in suffering.

III.B. Secondly, the joy of Yahweh is our stronghold in suffering because it prunes us, it purifies us, it stripes us, of all but Christ. Underlying this second point—and, indeed, underlying any joy the believer has in the midst of suffering, is God's absolute sovereignty. For if our suffering were merely the result of the randomness of nature or the happenstance of men's evil desires, then they would quickly unravel into purposelessness, and therefore meaninglessness, and therefore despairing madness. On in the hands of a Master Craftsmen can we have any hope of purpose and, therefore, any hope of joy.

And the Bible is empathically clear that God is the absolute sovereign author of everything that was, is, and is to come; what He wills, He does: "'for I am God, and there is no other; I am God, and there is none like Me, declaring the end from the beginning and from ancient times things not yet done, saying, "My counsel shall stand, and I will accomplish all My purpose"'" (Is. 46:9-10). He watches over His word to perform it (Jer. 1:12), and no purpose of His can be thwarted (Job 42:4; Ecc. 7:13). "All the inhabitants of the earth are reputed as nothing; He does according to His will in the army of heaven and among the inhabitants of the earth. No one can restrain His hand or say to Him, 'What have You done?'" (Dan. 4:35). "All that Yahweh pleased He has done—in the heavens and in earth, in the seas and all deep places" (Ps. 135:6 NYLT) as He "works all things according to the counsel of His will" (Eph. 1:11).

God is therefore the absolutely sovereign author of every detail pertaining to all things, including but not limited to wind (Lk. 8:25), lightning (Job 36:32), earthquakes (Acts 16:26; Rev. 16:18), snow (Ps. 147:16), frogs (Ex. 8:1-15), gnats (Ex. 8:16-19), flies (Ex. 8:20-32), locusts (Ex. 10:1-12), quail (Ex. 16:6-8), worms (Jonah 4:7), fish (Jonah 2:10), sparrows (Matt. 10:29), grass (Ps. 147:8), plants (Jonah 4:6), famine (Ps. 105:16), the sun (Josh. 10:12-13), prison doors (Acts 5:19), blindness (Ex. 4:11; Lk. 18:42), deafness (Ex. 4:11; Mk. 7:37), paralysis (Lk. 5:24-25), fever (Matt. 8:15), the sickness of children (2 Sam. 12:15), every disease (Matt. 4:23), travel plans (Jac. 4:13-15), the rolling of dice (Prov. 16:33), the loss or gain of money (1 Sam. 2:7), the hearts of kings (Prov. 21:1; Dan. 2:21), nations (Ps. 33:10), murderers (Acts 4:27-28), spiritual deadness (Eph. 2:4-5), the slaughter of His people (Ps. 44:11), the suffering of His saints (1 Pet. 4:19), the persecution of His children (Heb. 12:4-7), the repentance of souls (2 Tim. 2:25), the gift of faith (Phil. 1:29), the pursuit of holiness (Phil. 3:12-13), the maturity of the elect (Heb. 6:3), the giving of life and taking in death (1 Sam. 2:6), and the crucifixion of His Son (Acts 4:27-28).

Consequently, the suffering and sorrow of God's elect do not rest upon chance nor upon the will of men, but solely upon God's sovereign authorship—for He has appointed who shall suffer (Rev. 6:11), when they shall suffer (Jn. 7:30; Acts 18:9-10), where they shall suffer (Lk. 9:30, 13:33), and what kind of sufferings they shall experience (Mk. 9:13; Jn. 21:19; Acts 9:16, 13:29)—who among them shall die of hunger, with the sword, be lead into captivity, and be eaten up of beasts (Jer. 15:2-3). The saints of God, therefore, are immortal until their work is done (Ps. 139:16; Heb. 9:27; Jas. 4:13-16).

Consequently, suffering for the believer is a gift from God. That is what Paul told the church at Philippi: "For to you it has been granted on behalf of Christ, not only to believe in Him, but also to suffer for His sake" (Phil. 1:29). Peter boldly declares that we "suffer according to the will of God" (1 Pet. 4:19; see also 3:17). Elsewhere Peter tells us that we are called by God to suffer (1 Pet. 2:21; 3:9). Therefore, all suffering and sorrow, pain and grief is a gift from God. A calling by God. Willed by God. Why? There are more reasons to our suffering than we can presently imagine, and we will never fully know the reasons why this side of heaven.

But Scripture is clear that—with the very same love with which He loves His Son—God the Father orchestrates all of our suffering in order to prune us, refine us, and strip us of all but Christ. Yes, it is to make us holy (Rom. 5:1-5; Heb. 12:3-11; 2 Pet. 1:5-9). But holiness is never the end in and of itself. Rather, it is so that we might find full and lasting satisfaction in Christ as our treasure. People often say that God will never give them more than they can bear; that God entrusts them with their suffering because He knows that they can handle it. That's blasphemous.

Rather, the Christian responds as the Apostle Paul does in 2 Corinthians 12::

> [7] And that I might not be exalted overmuch by the exceeding greatness of the revelations, there was given to me a thorn in the flesh, a messenger of the Adversary, that he might buffet me, that I might not be exalted overmuch. [8] Concerning this thing I did call upon the Lord three times that it might depart from me. [9] And He said to me, "My grace is sufficient for you, for My power is perfected in infirmity." Most gladly, therefore, will I rather boast in my infirmities, that the power of the Messiah may rest on me. [10] Wherefore I am well pleased in infirmities, in mistreatments, in necessities, in persecutions, in distresses —for Messiah; for whenever I am infirm, then I am powerful.
>
> (2 Cor. 12:7-10 NYLT)

God's strength is made perfect in our weakness. In our sufferings. In our pain. God is most glorified when, truly, all we have is Christ. When He is our desire. Our delight. Our joy. Our treasure. Therefore most gladly will we boast in our pain and suffering, sorrows and grief, for when we are nothing, then Christ is magnified. When Christ is more precious to us than anything life has to offer or that death can take away, then He is most glorified.

This is the secret of the Christian life—contentment in Christ. We see this illustrated in Philippians, chapter 4:

> 11 Not that I say it in respect of want, for I did learn in things in which I am to be content. 12 I have known both to be humbled and I have known to abound. In everything and in all things I have learned the initiation secret both to be full and to be hungry, both to abound and to be in want. 13 For in all things I have strength in Messiah's strengthening me.
>
> (Phil. 4:11-13 NYLT)

The key, therefore, to being "sorrowful, yet always rejoicing" (2 Cor. 6:10) is that Christ is all we have. That He is more precious than all we could ever have. That He is more valuable than all we could ever lose. And therefore we can be content with nothing or with everything because Christ is our all in all. He is our life. The point of suffering is to drive us to Christ, to know Him intimately (Job 42:5), and therefore the more we treasure Him in our suffering, the more joy we have in our suffering. Only joy in Christ can make suffering pleasurable.

III.C. Third and finally, the joy in Yahweh is our stronghold in suffering because we magnify Christ's worth to the world. This builds on the point just made. Suffering not only internally strips us of everything but Christ, but then in living out that reality in the midst of suffering is a vibrant, living testimony to the beauty of Christ to others.

In Colossians, chapter 1, the Apostle Paul writes:

I now rejoice in my sufferings for you, and
fill up in my flesh the things lacking of the
tribulations of the Messiah for His body,
which is the assembly.

(Col. 1:24 NYLT)

What does Paul mean here when he says he "fill[s] up
in my flesh the things lacking of the tribulations of the
Messiah"?   We know he isn't saying that Christ's
atonement on the Cross was somehow deficient, for Christ
Himself said that "'It is finished'" (Jn. 19:30) upon Calvary's
hill.   Therefore we know Paul isn't saying that he is
somehow suffering to save people from sin and death, for
the author of Hebrews tells us that "Christ was offered
once to bear the sins of many" (Heb. 9:28).   There is only
one final and completed sacrifice for sins—Jesus Christ
upon the cross.

So we know what Paul doesn't mean, but the question
still remains as to what he does mean.   Paul uses nearly
identical language in Philippians 2:30 in commending
Epaphroditus to the church at Philippi for his sacrifices in
ministering to Paul in prison in Rome: "because for the
work of Christ he came close to death, not regarding his
life, to supply what was lacking in your service to me."
What was lacking in the ministry of the Philippian church to
Paul?   Nothing but a visible manifestation of that service.
In other words, they couldn't all go to Rome to serve Paul,
so they sent Epaphroditus to Paul as their representative
to show Paul how much they love and care for him.

That is precisely what Paul is saying in Colossians
1:24.   Not that Christ's sufferings and death were
insufficient, but rather that Paul, in his own sufferings and
pending martyrdom, is visibly demonstrating to those who
never witnessed the horror of Calvary what the glory and

117

worth of the love of God is. A pain-free life doesn't show anybody the love of Christ. Joyless sorrow in the midst of heartache doesn't show anybody the love of Christ. Rather, what the world needs most is the infinite value of the love of God by how Christians are "sorrowful, yet always rejoicing" (2 Cor. 6:10). It is only when we show that Christ is our treasure in good times and bad, in carefree days and when the floor gives way beneath us, when we have everything and when we have nothing, that they will want what—or, more accurately, Who—we have.

Concluding Implications:

I conclude with a portion of the funeral sermon given by George Muller, a famous 19th century pastor, upon his wife's death:

> The last portion of scripture which I read to my precious wife was this: "The Lord God is a sun and shield, the Lord will give grace and glory, no good thing will he withhold from them that walk uprightly." Now, if we have believed in the Lord Jesus Christ, we have received grace, we are partakers of grace, and to all such he will give glory also. I said to myself, with regard to the latter part, "no good thing will he withhold from them that walk uprightly"—I am in myself a poor worthless sinner, but I have been saved by the blood of Christ; and I do not live in sin, I walk uprightly before God. Therefore, if it is really good for me, my darling wife will be raised up again; sick as she is. God will

> restore her again. But if she is not restored again, then it would not be a good thing for me [to have her]. And so my heart was at rest. I was satisfied with God. And all this springs, as I have often said before, from taking God at his word, believing what he says.

Look at what he said—he is satisfied in God because he knows that God will only do what is good, what is best, for him because he is clothed with Christ's righteousness.

Or, to put it another way, all of our grief and sorrow, pain and suffering, are blood-bought gifts purchased by Christ on Calvary for they are blessings and privileges designed by God for our good and joy. Therefore, if God sacrificed His one and only Son to obtain them, then they must be necessary for my joy in treasuring Him supremely.

Or, to put it another way, the only troubles that God permits in the lives of His children are those that will bring more pleasure than trouble with them—when all things are considered.

Or, to put it in yet a final way, if we suffer it is because God values something in us greater than our physical comfort and health that He in His infinite wisdom and kindness knows can only be attained by means of our physical affliction and the lessons of submission and dependency and trust in Him that we learn from it.

Therefore, with George Muller who found much comfort in this hymn, let us sing:

> Best of blessings He'll provide us
> Nought but good shall e'er betide us,
> Safe to glory He will guide us,
> Oh how He loves!

Or let us sing with the hymn *On Christ the Solid Rock I Stand*:

> His oath, His covenant, His blood,
> Support me in the whelming flood.
> When all around my soul gives way,
> He then is all my Hope and Stay.

Let us kiss Christ—the Rose of Sharon—even in the midst of the thorns as we sing:

> [1] In Jesus I found such a wonderful friend,
> He satisfies all of my need;
> He's more than my heart ever could comprehend,
> O He is a Savior indeed.

> Chorus:
> He is the rose of Sharon,
> Fragrant and sweet to me,
> He is my light when shadows fall,
> Savior and keeper is He;
> He is the rose of Sharon,
> He is my all in all.

> [2] My constant Companion, my Counselor too,
> My High Priest most holy is He;
> The King of my soul and my Advocate true,
> My Savior forever will be. [Chorus]

3 Far more than the trifles that earth can afford,
In Christ my Redeemer I see;
In Him all the treasures of Heaven are stored,
Eternal His praises shall be. [Chorus]

NATHAN W. TUCKER

6 THIS IS THE DAY THAT YAHWEH HAS MADE

*I*n this chapter I want to continue to look at God's providence in a believer's pain and suffering. In the last chapter I only briefly touched on the possible reasons why God does what He does, and believe that the topic is incomplete without a further examination into His Providence.

I. **Defining Providence.** But what do I mean by the term *Providence*? The word is used no where in most English versions of the Bible. My dictionary defines it as "the protective care of God." It is built upon the word *provide*, which comes from two Latin words: *pre* (which means *forward* or *on behalf of*) and *vide* (*to see*). An English idiom that captures the idea of the Latin origins of providence is, "I will see to it." Literally, therefore, providence means "to supply what is needed."

How has the Church historically defined God's Providence? In Question 27 (week 10) the Heidelberg Catechism (1563) asks, "What do you understand by the providence of God?" It answers as follows:

> God's Providence is His almighty and ever present power, whereby, as with His hand, He still upholds heaven and earth and all creatures, and so governs them that leaf and blade, rain and drought, fruitful and barren years, food and drink, health and sickness, riches and poverty, indeed, all things, come to us not by chance but by His fatherly hand.

Notice, first, that the Heidelberg Catechism grounds Providence in God's "almighty and ever present power" over all things, and then, secondly, that He directs such power "by His fatherly hand." The foundation for God's Providence is His absolute sovereignty, and then Providence describes *how*, or *why*, He wields His absolute sovereignty.

The Belgic Confession (1561) defines Providence in Article 13 as:

> We believe that the same God, after He had created all things, did not forsake them, or give them up to fortune or chance, but that He rules and governs them according to His holy will, so that nothing happens in this world without His appointment...

Notice, again, that the Belgic Confession grounds God's Providence in His absolute sovereignty in ruling and governing all things He had created so that nothing happens by "fortune or chance." Then the Confession defines God's Providence as how He exercises such power—the appointing all things by "His holy will."

Question 18 of the Westminster Larger Catechism (1648) asks, "What are God's works of Providence?" The answer it provides is that:

> God's works of Providence are His most holy, wise, and powerful preserving and governing all His creatures; ordering them, and all their actions, to His own glory.

Once again the foundation for God's Providence is His absolute sovereignty in "preserving and governing all His creatures; ordering them, and all their actions." Then the Catechism defines God's Providence as *how* He wields such power—by His holiness and wisdom for His own glory.

Finally, we come to the Second London Baptist Confession of Faith (1689), which in Chapter 5, section 1, defines God's Providence as follows:

> God the good Creator of all things, in His infinite power and wisdom, upholds, directs, arranges, and governs all creatures and things, from the greatest to the least, by His perfectly wise and holy providence, to the purpose for which they were created. He governs according to His infallible foreknowledge and the free and unchangeable counsel of His own will. His providence leads to the praise of the glory of His wisdom, power, justice, infinite goodness, and mercy.

Once again we see that the basis of God's Providence is His absolute sovereignty—"His infinite power" by which He "upholds, directs, arranges, and governs all creatures and things, from the greatest to the least." Then Providence builds upon this foundation—describing *how* God exercises His power: as "the good Creator of all things, in His infinite...wisdom...by His perfectly wise and holy [counsel]...to the praise of the glory of His wisdom, power, justice, infinite goodness, and mercy."

In conclusion, therefore, God's Providence has been understood by the Church throughout the centuries as:

(a) the infinitely and perfectly good, wise, and holy exercise,

(b) of His absolute sovereignty,

(c) to the praise of His glory.

II. God's Absolute Sovereignty. Let us dwell for a few moments on God's absolute sovereignty, for without it there is no such thing as God's Providence but mere divine wishful thinking. There is no such thing as God's fatherly care, but mere paternal impotence. God's infinite and perfect power is the foundation upon which God's Providence is built; the hinge upon which the entire edifice swings wide open to comfort and encourage God's children.

God is the unescapable essence of all reality, for the Apostle Paul declares, "For of Him and through Him and to Him are all things, to whom be glory forever! Amen!" (Rom. 11:36). In Colossians, the Apostle tells us that:

> [16] because in Him were created all things in the heavens and upon the earth—the visible and the invisible—whether thrones, whether lordships, whether principalities, whether authorities. All things have been created through Him and for Him. [17] And He is before all, and in Him all things have stood together.
>
> (Col. 1:16-17 NYLT)

Notice the last part of that last verse—"in Him all things have stood together." In God all the universe is held together every single second of every single day. Nothing occurs, therefore, that He did not cause. And, as the author of Hebrews tells us, God is the One, "for whom are all things and by whom are all things" (Heb. 2:10). God causes all things for His own glory. Let's look at five categories of events that the Bible makes clear that God is the absolutely sovereign author of.

II.A. Sovereign Over So-Called "Gods." First, the Bible tells us that God is not only the absolute sovereign Ruler over the so-called "gods" of this world, but that He delights in bringing judgment upon them as well. In Exodus, for instance, God declared that He had judged all the gods of Egypt by killing all of the firstborn—whether of man or of beast—in the land (Ex. 12:12). When the Philistines captured the Ark of the Covenant, God caused the statue of the Philistine god Dagon to fall on its face before the Ark of the Covenant with its head and hands broken off (1 Sam. 5:1-5). In the book of Isaiah God mocks His backsliding people Israel for seeking after other gods, saying, "'When you cry out, let your collection of idols deliver you. But the wind will carry them all away; a breath will take them'" (Is. 57:13). In contrast, however, the Bible declares, "Blessed are all those who put their trust in [God]" (Ps. 2:12).

God is the ultimate and eternal Supreme Being of which nothing greater can be conceived. There cannot be two or more Supreme Beings for the simple reason that neither one of them would therefore be supreme. There can only be one Great I Am—the uncreated, self-sufficient, self-existent, unchangeable, limitless One who has no beginning, no end, no need, and no weakness (Ex. 3:14-15; Numb. 23:19; Ps. 33:11, 102:27; Mal. 3:6; Jn. 5:26; Heb. 13:8; James 1:17; Rev.1:8, 22:13). He is the uncreated source of all created things who does not owe His existence to anyone or anything else.

And because God is the all-powerful sovereign of the universe, He has no rival. Period. For the Bible declares, "And you have known today, and have turned it back unto your heart, that Yahweh, He is God—in the heavens above, and on the earth beneath—there is none else" (Deut. 4:39 NYLT; see also Deut. 4:35, 6:4-5, 32:39a; 2 Kings 5:16; Is. 45:22; Joel 2:27). All angels and demons, spirits and so-called "gods," have beginnings, are bound by physical locations, and have their power limited by some outside constraint. Even the devil himself is but one of God's creatures who can do nothing without God's permission. Satan has been described in Scripture as "the ruler of this world" (John 12:31, 14:30; 1 Jn. 5:19), "the god of this word" (2 Cor. 4:4; Eph. 2:1-2), and as a "roaring lion prowling about, seeking whom he may devour" (1 Pet. 5:8). But the Bible is also clear that he has to seek permission from God to do anything (Job 1:12, 2:6; Mk. 1:27; Lk. 4:6, 22:31-32, 53) and that his doom is sure (Jn. 16:11; Rev. 20:10).

II.B. **Sovereign Over Nature.** God is not only the absolute sovereign Ruler over (1) all other so-called "gods," but He is (2) the absolute sovereign over every detail pertaining to the natural world. For instance, in Luke, chapter 8, we read:

> 22 And it came to pass, on one of the days, that He Himself went into a boat with His disciples, and He said unto them, "We may go over to the other side of the lake." And they set forth. 23 And as they are sailing He fell asleep. And there came down a windstorm on the lake, and they were filling with water, and were in peril.

AGAPE: THE ESSENCE OF SAVING FAITH

> 24 And having come near, they awoke
> Him, saying, "Master, master, we perish!"
> And He, having arisen, rebuked the wind
> and the raging of the water. And they
> ceased, and there came a calm. 25 But he
> said to them, "Where is your faith?" And
> they, being afraid, marveled, saying to one
> another, "Who, then, is this, that He
> commands even the winds and the water
> and they obey Him?"
>
> (Lk. 8:22-25 NYLT)

Jesus "rebuked the wind and the raging of the water. And they ceased, and there was calm" (vs. 24). And His disciples, "being afraid, marveled, saying to one another, 'Who, then, is this, that He commands even the winds and the water and they obey Him?" (vs. 25).

In the book of Jonah, we read that "Yahweh appoints a great fish to shallow up Jonah" (Jonah 1:16 NYLT) as the reluctant prophet attempt to "flee from the face of Yahweh" (vs. 3 NYLT). After being "in the bowels of the fish three days and three nights," (vs. 17 NYLT), "Yahweh speaks to the fish, and it vomits Jonah out onto dry land (2:10 NYLT). Later, we are told "Yahweh God appoints a vine and causes it to come up over Jonah, to be a shade over his head to give deliverance from his affliction" (4:6 NYTL). "But God appoints a worm at the going up of the dawn on the next day, and it smites the worm and dries it up" (vs. 7 NYLT).

In the Gospel of Matthew, the Lord Christ tells us that, though "two sparrows are sold for a penny, yet not one of them will fall to the ground apart from the will of" God (Matt. 10:29). The Bible makes clear that God is the sovereign Ruler over all nature, authoring and designing

129

every detail of His creation, from the wind (Lk. 8:35) to lightning (Job. 36:32), earthquakes (Acts 16:26; Rev. 16:18), snow (Ps. 147:18), frogs (Ex. 8:1-15), gnats (Ex. 8:16-19), flies (Ex. 8:20-32), locusts (Ex. 10:1-12), quail (Ex. 16:6-8), worms (Jonah 4:7), fish (Jonah 2:10), sparrows (Matt. 10:29), grass (Ps. 147:8), plants (Jonah 4:6), famine (Ps. 105:16), the sun (Josh. 10:12-13), and everything else in the entire universe.

II.C.   Sovereign Over Man.   Not only is God the absolute, sovereign Ruler over (1) all other so-called "gods," and (2) the natural world, but also (3) of the affairs of men as well. For Proverbs tells us that though, "the lot is cast into the center, all its judgment is from Yahweh" (Prov. 16:33 NYLT).   Hannah tells us that, "Yahweh dispossesses, and He makes rich; He makes low, indeed, He makes high" (1 Sam. 2:7 NYLT).   Scripture makes clear that, "The heart of a king is like channels of waters in the hand of Yahweh; He inclines it wherever He pleases" (Prov. 21:1 NYLT). In the book of Daniel we read that, "He changes times and seasons; He sets up kings and deposes them.   He gives wisdom to the wise and knowledge to the discerning" (Dan. 2:21; see also Lk. 1:52). The psalmist declares that, "Yahweh made void the counsel of nations; He forbid the thoughts of the peoples" (Ps. 33:10 NYLT).   Even men's travel plans belong to the Lord (Jac. 4:13-17).

Because God is sovereign, it also necessarily implies that He is not only all-powerful, but also all-knowing.   In Isaiah, God declares, "'See, the former things have taken place, and new things I declare'" (Is. 42:8). A few chapters later, God proclaims, "'I make known the end from the beginning, from ancient times what is still to come'" (Is. 46:10; see also Is. 44:7).   The psalmist praises God by saying, "⁴For there is not a word on my tongue that, behold!—O Yahweh, You know it all!...¹⁶Your eyes saw my unformed substance, and all the days formed for me are written on Your scroll when as yet there was not one among them!" (Ps. 139:4, 16). Before the universe was formed and time even began, God had already orchestrated every detail of every second of history, and nothing will prevent Him from bringing it about (Job 42:2; Ecc. 3:13; Lk. 1:37).

II.D.   Sovereign Over Evil.   Not only is God the absolute, sovereign Ruler over (1) all other so-called "gods," (2) the natural world, (3) of the affairs of men, but (4) this absolute sovereign authorship extends even to evil, to all the suffering and sorrow in the world.   For in Deuteronomy God has declared, "'See now that I Myself am [God]! There is no god beside Me! I put to death and I bring to life. I have wounded and I will heal. And no one can deliver out My hand'" (Deut. 32:39).   In Exodus God proclaims, "'...Who appointed a mouth for man?   Or who appoints the mute or deaf, or open-eyed or blind? Is it not I, Yahweh?'" (Ex. 4:11 NYLT). God, therefore, is ultimately the One who puts to death and who causes new birth, who heals and who wounds, who makes some deaf and mute, or makes some blind or able to see.

God designs evil (Gen. 50:20; Ps. 105:17) and affliction (Ruth 1:20-21; Job 42:11), so that, if a calamity occurs in a city, only He has ultimately done it (Amos 3:6). Yahweh gives and Yahweh takes away (Job 1:21), He gives good as well as evil (Job 2:10; Jn. 3:27; 1 Cor. 4:7). He therefore is the absolute sovereign author of the barrenness of the womb (Gen. 4:1, 16:2, 20:18, 25:21, 29:31, 30:2; 1 Sam. 1:5-6, 2:5-6; Ruth 4:113), sickness of children (2 Sam. 12:15), fever (Matt. 8:15), paralysis (Lk.

5:24-25), blindness (Ex. 4:11; Lk. 18:42), deafness (Ex. 4:11; Mk. 7:37), and every other possible ailment (Matt. 4:23).

As a result of the first man Adam's initial sin, the Bible declares that all "creation waits in eager expectation" (Rom. 8:19) to be regenerated at Christ's second coming (Matt. 19:28). We see this in Romans, chapter 8:

> [20] for to vanity was the creation made subject, not of its will, but because of Him who did subject it in hope [21] that also the creation itself shall be set free from its slavery to corruption into the liberty of the glory of the children of God. [22] For we have known that all creation groans together and travails in pain together till now.
>
> (Rom. 8:20-22 NYLT)

II.E.   Sovereign over Sin.   Not only is God the absolute, sovereign Ruler over (1) all other so-called "gods," (2) the natural world, (3) of the affairs of men, (4) evil, but (5) and finally, this absolute sovereign authorship extends even to sin itself. In this section we'll briefly look at just two examples from Scripture.

II.E.1. The first comes from Genesis 20, where we read that Abraham and his wife Sarah traveled to the city of Gerar:

> [1] And Abraham journeys from there toward the land of the South, and dwells between Kadesh and Shur, and sojourns in Gerar.

2 Now Abraham says concerning Sarah his wife, "She is my sister." And Abimelech king of Gerar sends and takes Sarah.

3 But God comes in unto Abimelech in a dream of the night, and says to him, "Behold!—you are a dead man because of the woman whom you have taken, for she is married to a husband."

4 But Abimelech has not drawn near unto her; and he says "Adonai, will You slay a righteous nation also? 5 Has he himself not said to me, 'She is my sister'? And she, even she herself, said, 'He is my brother.' In the integrity of my heart, and in the innocence of my hands, I have done this."

6 And God says unto him in the dream, "Yes, I have known that in the integrity of your heart you have done this, for I withhold you, even I, from sinning against Me; therefore I have not suffered you to come against her. 7 And now send back the man's wife, for he is a prophet, and he prays for you, and you shall live. But if you do not send her back, know that dying you die, you and all that you have."

(Gen. 20:1-7 NYLT)

Notice what God tells Abimelech when he protests that he was acting in "the integrity of my heart, and in the innocence of my hands" because he had innocently relied upon Abraham's deception (vs. 5 NYLT). God replied that, "Yes, I have known that in the integrity of your heart you have done this, *for I withhold you, even I, from sinning against Me; therefore I have not suffered you to come against her*" (vs. 6 NYLT (emphasis added)).   Let me repeat that, God told Abimelech that the only reason he did not commit the sin of adultery was because *God* restrained him from it.

And if God is able to keep Abimelech from sinning, is He not therefore able to keep everyone from sinning at all times and in all places?   In fact, we know that in heaven there is no sin because God graciously enables it's citizens to perfectly love Yahweh their God with all their hearts, soul, mind, and body.   Therefore, if God is able to keep Abimelech from sinning, and the inhabitants of heaven from sinning, then He is perfectly capable of prohibiting all sin altogether.   But He doesn't.   Rather, He decrees it for His holy purposes.

II.E.2. We could look at the example of Eli's sons in 1 Kings 2 who God desired to kill for their wickedness and therefore He did not restrain their evil as He did Abimelech. Or we could look at the example of Pharaoh in Exodus whose heart God hardened to display His glory.   Instead, however, we will look secondly at the crucifixion of God the Son.   For the Bible makes clear that long before time began, in ages past before He created the world (Gen. 1-2) and the first man fell (Gen. 3), He decreed (Acts 2:23, 4:28; 1 Cor. 2:7) that He would make a name for Himself (Ezek. 38:23) by redeeming a people for Himself (Eph. 1:4; Tit. 2:14; 1 Pet. 2:9-10) by the sacrifice of Himself (Rom. 3:25) in the incarnate God-man Jesus Christ.

Turn with me to Acts, chapter 4, the passage that not only made me a believer but a lover of the absolute sovereignty of God.   For in it we find that God the Father

decreed in eternity past when, where, how, and by whom
God the Son would be killed:

> 27 "For truly gathered together against
> Your holy Servant Jesus, whom You
> anointed, were both Herod and Pontius
> Pilate, with the ethnic groups and peoples
> of Israel, 28 to do whatever Your hand and
> Your counsel determined beforehand to
> come to pass."
>
> (Acts 4:27-28 NYLT)

Look at all the human actors responsible—yes, morally
culpable before God—for the death of the Lord Christ: (a)
King Herod, (b) the Roman governor Pontius Pilate, (c) the
Gentile solders, and (d) the Jewish people (vs. 27).   But
even though these human actors are guilty of perpetrating
the greatest evil in the history of the world—the crucifixion
of God the Son—verse 28 tells us that they merely did
"whatever Your hand and Your purpose determined
beforehand to come to pass" (NYLT). In other words, God
decreed or preordained this evil down to the minutest
detail, and these human actors were simply executing
God's will.

In the 53rd chapter of Isaiah we see even more
explicitly that God the Father decreed the most evil act
imaginable in the crucifixion of God the Son:

> 3 "He is despised, and discarded of men,
> A man of pains, and acquainted with
> suffering,
> And as one hiding the face from us, He is
> despised, and we esteemed Him not.
> 4 Surely our sicknesses he has borne,

And our pains—He has carried them,
And we—we have esteemed Him plagued,
smitten of God, and afflicted.
5 And He is pierced for our transgressions,
Bruised for our iniquities,
The chastisement of our peace is on Him,
And by his bruise there is healing to us.
6 All of us like sheep have wandered,
Each to his own way we have turned,
And Yahweh has laid on Him the
punishment of us all.
7 He was oppressed and He was afflicted,
Yet He opens not his mouth,
As a lamb to the slaughter He is brought,
And as a sheep before its shearers is
dumb,
So He opens not his mouth.
8 By restraint and by judgment He has
been taken,
And of His generation who meditates—
That He has been cut off from the land of
the living?
By the transgression of My people He is
plagued.
9 And His grave is appointed with the
wicked,
And with the rich at His death,
Because He has done no violence,
Nor is deceit in His mouth.
10 And Yahweh has delighted to bruise
Him,
He has made Him suffer,
If His soul makes an offering for guilt,
He sees His seed -- He prolongs His days,

And the pleasure of Yahweh prospers in
His hand.
[11] Of the labor of His soul He sees—and is
satisfied,
Through His knowledge the righteous
One, My Servant, gives righteousness to
many,
And their iniquities He bears.
[12] Therefore I give a portion to Him among
the great,
And He apportions spoil with the mighty,
Because He exposed His soul to death,
And with transgressors He was numbered,
And the sin of many He has borne,
And for transgressors He intercedes."

(Is. 53:3-12 NYLT)

God the Son was smitten by God the Father and
afflicted (vs. 4). It delighted God the Father to bruise the
Lord Christ and to make Him suffer (vs. 10). God the
Father made His one and only Son an offering for sin by
laying upon Him the iniquity of His elect (vs. 6, 10).
Therefore, if a holy and righteous God—infinitely, eternally,
and perfectly so—decreed this, the greatest of all evils,
then it stands to reason that He is also the absolute
sovereign of all other sins as well.

As we conclude our examination of God's sovereignty,
we have seen that the Bible makes it absolutely,
unequivocally clear that God decrees every detail of every
second of all of history in the entire universe. God the
absolute, sovereign Ruler over (1) all other so-called
"gods," (2) the natural world, (3) of the affairs of men, (4)
evil, and (5) sin itself.

And by absolute sovereignty, Scripture means that God is the author of everything. He fashions it, designs it, controls it, and wills it to happen to accomplish His purposes.[2] As King Nebuchadnezzar of Babylon exclaimed:

> [34] "...and the Most High I have blessed,
> and the Age-enduring Living One I have praised and honored,
> Whose dominion is an age-enduring dominion,
> And His kingdom is from generation and generation.
> [35] And all who are dwelling on the earth are reckoned as nothing;
> And He does according to His will among the strength
> Of the heavens and those dwelling on the earth.
> And there is none that strikes His hand
> And says to Him, 'What has You done?'"
>   (Dan. 4:34b-35 NYLT)

As author A.W. Pink wrote in his book *The Sovereignty of God*, "The sovereignty of the God of Scripture is absolute, irresistible, infinite." As the psalmist declares in Psalm 135:

---

[2] This does not preclude, of course, God's use of second causes (Gen. 8:22; Is. 55:10-11; Acts 27:31-44), though He is free to work without (Hos. 1:7), above (Rom. 4:19-21), and against them (Dan. 3:17) at His pleasure.

[5] For I have known that Yahweh is great,
Yes, our Adonai is above all gods.
[6] All that Yahweh pleased He has done,
In the heavens and in earth,
In the seas and all deep places,

(Psalm 135:5-6 NYLT)

III. God's Providence. Now that we have established the foundation of God's absolute sovereignty, we can now build upon it the house of God's Providence.

III.A. Providence is not Fate. First, however, we must differentiate Providence from the the ancient Greek idea of fate. Here is how the famous 19th century Baptist pastor Charles Spurgeon distinguished the two in a sermon entitled God's Providence:

> I believe that every particle of dust that dances in the sunbeam does not move an atom more or less than God wishes—that every particle of spray that dashes against the steamboat has its orbit as well as the sun in the heavens—that the chaff from the hand of the winnower is steered as the stars in their courses. The creeping of an aphid over the rosebud is as much fixed as the march of the devastating pestilence —the fall of...leaves from a poplar is as fully ordained as the tumbling of an avalanche...
>
> You will say this morning, Our minister is a fatalist. Your minister is no such thing. Some will say, Ah! he believes in fate. He does not believe in fate at all. What is

fate? Fate is this—whatever is, must be. But there is a difference between that and providence. Providence says, "Whatever God ordains must be."

But the wisdom of God never ordains anything without purpose. Everything in this world is working for some great end. Fate does not say that. Fate simply says that the thing must be; Providence says, God moves the wheels along, and there they are...

There is all the difference between fate and province as there is between a man with good eyes and a blind man. He who has faith is better than the stoic. The stoical philosopher bore it because he believed it must be. The Christian bears it because he believes it is working for his good.

Fate, therefore, is purposeless, and therefore without meaning, and therefore full of hopelessness and despair. Providence, however, is purposeful, and therefore meaningful, and therefore hopeful and endurable.

III.B. Providence Provides Hope. This leads to the our second point—understanding the doctrine of Providence is essential for the Christian to bear up under sorrow and grief. For instance, Question 28 of the Heidelberg Catechism asks, "What does it benefit us to know that God has created all things and still upholds them by His providence?" The answer it provides reads:

> [So that] we can be patient in adversity, thankful in prosperity, and with a view to the future we can have a firm confidence in our faithful God and Father that no creature shall separate us from his love; for all creatures are so completely in his hand that without his will they cannot so much as move.

It is so that "we can be patient in adversity, thankful in prosperity, and with a view to the future we can have a firm confidence in our faithful God and Father." That is why understanding Providence is so important. Or as Article 13 of the Belgic Confession states:

> This doctrine affords us unspeakable consolation, since we are taught thereby that nothing can befall us by chance, but by the direction of our most gracious and heavenly Father; who watches over us with a paternal care, keeping all creatures so under His power, that not a hair of our head (for they are all numbered), nor a sparrow, can fall to the ground, without the will of our Father, in whom we do entirely trust; being persuaded, that He so restrains the devil and all our enemies, that without His will and permission, they cannot hurt us.

"This doctrine affords us unspeakable consolation" because all things happen to us, not by chance, but by the "paternal care" of "our most gracious and heavenly Father."

There is a theory called the butterfly effect, made famous a few years ago by a movie of the same name. It holds that the flap of the wings of a single butterfly, for instance, can have massive but untold repercussions (such as altering the path of a distant storm). Imagine then, if you will, all the countless ripple effects caused in just a single half second of human history the world over. And the butterfly effect is not merely limited to the physical realm, but naturally extends to all social interactions as well.

But let's apply this theory to every single event in every single second in all of human history. Either they are random, meaningless brain farts of the universe, or they are plotted down to the exactest detail by the Master Storyteller. There can be no in-between. God cannot be partially sovereign—planning, for instance, just a few events in human history here and there. For such sporadic Providence would render Him completely incapable of keeping His story from unraveling due to all the unintended butterfly effects He carelessly causes as He intervenes on ad ad hoc basis in human history. God must be completely sovereign, or incompetent.

Only an absolutely sovereign God can orchestrate such seeming chaos that we see throughout the world. Therefore, the wisdom of the God of the Bible can be trusted precisely because He is the Potter rather than a blunderer. The promises of the God of the Bible can be trusted precisely because He is sovereign rather than impotent. The Providence of the God of the Bible can be trusted precisely because He is the Grand Weaver rather than a synergistic tailor. The goodness of the God of the Bible can be trusted precisely because there is no such thing as meaningless pain and suffering.

That is what the doctrine of God's Providence, grounded in absolute sovereignty, is all about—hope that endures, come what may.

III.C. Providence Tests, Strengthens, & Purifies Faith.
Third and finally, what are the promises of Providence that lead to hope?   It is hazardous, to try to discern all the reasons and outcomes God is orchestrating in any given event. A fatal car accident may at first seem evil, until the mortician discovers the victim had a yet-to-be diagnosed bone cancer that would have resulted in a very painful, years-long death.   Winning the lottery ticket may initially seem good, until it results in bankruptcy a ruined family, and broken friendships.

However, Scripture does, in broad strokes, explain why believers suffer from hardship and wrongdoing, pain and sorrow. 1 Peter, chapter 1, for instance, explains:

> [6] In this you greatly rejoice, though now for a little while, if it be necessary, you are being made sorrowful in various trials, [7] that the proof of your faith, being much more precious than gold that is perishing, is being proved through fire that it may be found to praise, and honor, and glory in the revelation of Jesus Messiah,[8] whom, not having seen, you agape.   In whom, though now not seeing, you are believing as you rejoice with joy inexpressible and glorified, [9] receiving the end of your faith— the salvation of you souls.
>
> (1 Pet. 1:6-9 NYLT)

That, in essence, is why believers grieve and suffer—so that their faith, which is far more precious than gold that perishes, will be tested, strengthened, and purified, that they might be saved and praised at the revelation of Jesus Christ. Every new trial that comes their way has been personally authored by the hand of an infinitely loving and merciful Father (Rom. 5:3-5; 1 Pet. 1:6-9, 5:10) for, as Scripture tells us:

(a) discipline that leads to repentance (Lk. 13:4-5);
(b) pruning that leads to abounding fruit (Jn. 15:1-8);
(c) humiliating weakness that severs our self-reliance (Deut. 8:3, 16; 2 Cor. 12::7-10; Phil. 3:7-16, 4:11-13).

And all this so that they may be partakers of His holiness (Heb. 12:10) and know Him intimately (Job 42:5).

God is most glorified by the indomitable though painful joy (Is. 43:3; Jn. 15:11, 17:13; Rom. 9:2-3; 2 Cor. 6:10) of His saints in Christ Jesus who, while in the very midst of suffering and sorrow, they in humble, gusty trust (Prov. 28:1; Acts 21:14; Heb. 4:16) continue to worship and bless His name (Job 1:20-21) and find their contentment in Him alone (Ps. 16:11, 21:6, 27:1-4, 42:1-2, 43:4, 63:1-5, 73:25-26; Hab. 3:17-18; Jn. 15:11, 16:24, 17:13; 1 Pet. 1:8; 1 Jn. 1:4). They magnify His beauty by kissing the Rose of Sharon while hallowing His thorns (Sons 2:1), declaring, "Go, then, earthly fame and treasure. Come disaster, scorn, and pain. In Your service, pain is pleasure. With Your favor, loss is gain" (Phil. 1:20-21, 3:7-11). By seeing faith they understand that God moves in mysterious ways (Job 5:9; Ecc. 3:11, 7:23, 8:17; Rom. 11:33); therefore, they judge Him not by feeble sense, but trust Him for His grace, for they are assured that behind a frowning providence He hides a smiling face (Rom. 8:28, 32; 2 Cor. 4:17). Though He slay them, yet they will trust Him (Job

13:15) and magnify Him, because for them to live is Christ and to die is gain (Eph. 2:7; Phil. 1:20-21).

There are an unsearchable number of good that God produces in but a single event that we will never see (Job 5:9; Ecc. 3:11, 7:23, 8:17; Rom. 11:33). But while we may never know all the "whys" this side of heaven, we can take comfort in the fact that each moment of each day contains a complex tapestry of innumerable deterministic chaoses (i.e., butterfly effects) that can only be weaved by His sovereign authorship (Prov. 8:22-31; Ecc. 3:1-8, 11; Acts 17:28; Rom. 8:28, 11:36; Col. 1:16-17; Heb. 1:3, 2:10).

Therefore—whatever may come, whatever each new day may bring—we can confidently declare with the psalmist in Psalm 118:24 that, "This is the day Yahweh has made; we rejoice and are glad in it!" (NYLT).

COMING SUMMER 2025!

YOU MUST BE BORN AGAIN!

AN EXPOSITION OF THE NECESSITY OF REGENERATION

OTHER BOOKS BY NATHAN TUCKER:

The Five Solas: An Expository Exhortation

Julia's Christmas Carol

Letters From Cell No. 73

Constitutional Musings: An Anthology of Legal Columns

We the People: The Only Cure to Judicial Activism